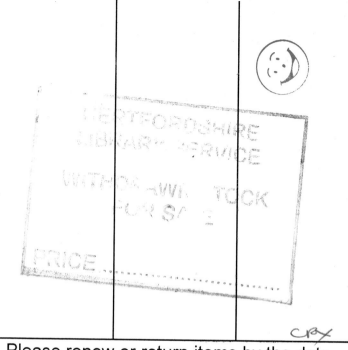
Please renew or return items by the date
shown on your receipt

www.hertsdirect.org/libraries

Renewals and
enquiries: 0300 123 4049

Textphone for hearing   0300 123 4041
or speech impaired

Other Pocket Essentials by this author:

Freud & Psychoanalysis
Roget – the Man Who Became a Book

Robin Hood

Myth, History and Culture

Nick Rennison

POCKET ESSENTIALS

First published in 2012 by Pocket Essentials,
an imprint of Oldcastle Books Ltd,
PO Box 394, Harpenden, Herts, AL5 1XJ
www.pocketessentials.com

A CIP catalogue record for this book is available from the British Library.

ISBN
978-1-84243-247-1 (print)
978-1-84243-636-3 (Kindle)
978-1-84243-637-0 (Epub)
978-1-84243-638-7 (PDF)

2 4 6 8 10 9 7 5 3 1

Typeset by Avocet Typeset, Chilton, Aylesbury, Bucks, HP18 9FG
in 9pt Univers Light
Printed in Great Britain by Clays Ltd, St Ives plc

Contents

Introduction

In Julian Barnes's satirical novel *England, England*, a media magnate who is intent on turning the Isle of Wight into one gigantic theme park celebrating 'Englishness' commissions his marketing men to come up with a list of the fifty subjects most associated with the word 'England'. Robin Hood and His Merrie Men comes seventh on the list, behind the Royal Family, Big Ben and Manchester United Football Club but well ahead of Shakespeare, Stonehenge and the Beefeaters at the Tower of London. Robin and Co duly become one of the theme park's most popular attractions. Barnes is, of course, exaggerating for comic effect but he is right in highlighting the continuing significance of the famous outlaw. More than six hundred years after he first appeared in a handful of medieval poems, he is a worldwide cultural figure who represents particular ideas about England and Englishness. Start looking for him and Robin Hood is everywhere. There are Robin Hood novels and Robin Hood films, Robin Hood comics and Robin Hood computer games. He can be found in TV series, operas, musicals, pantomimes, graphic novels, cartoons and comedy shows. As the scholar Lois Potter has written, 'it is difficult to find a medium in which Robin Hood has not been represented'. He is at the heart of a tourist industry in Nottinghamshire, the county which claims him as its own, and he has an airport named after him. His fame is such that mere mention of his name in a newspaper headline ensures that readers know what to expect from the story. Call a proposed fiscal measure a 'Robin Hood' tax, for example, and everyone knows what its redistributive aim will be.

The story of the 'good outlaw', the person who breaks the laws of the land but nonetheless epitomises a sense of fairness that is not necessarily encoded in those laws, is a familiar figure in many cultures. There are Robin Hood-like characters from around the world (Juraj Janosik in Slovakia, Chucho el Roto in Mexico, Kobus van der Schlossen in Holland) but there is only one Robin Hood. As hero, trickster and mythological embodiment of a justice beyond that of the law, he stands alone.

Because of his great fame, we assume we know who Robin Hood was. Ask people in the street about him and a composite picture of the outlaw will soon start to emerge. He lived in the time of Richard the Lionheart and Prince John. He was a man who returned from the Crusades and was driven into exile in the forest by the treachery of others. He was a Saxon who fought against the tyranny of the Normans. He was a nobleman reduced to poverty and outlawry by the loss of his lands, stolen from him by villains like the Sheriff of Nottingham. Accompanied by faithful comrades like Little John, Will Scarlet and Friar Tuck, he robbed the rich and gave to the poor. The love of his life was Maid Marian. Begin looking into the story of Robin Hood and you soon find that very little of this is true of the original outlaw of the medieval poems. The 'facts' about Robin Hood that everybody knows, those of his attributes with which people are most familiar, turn out to have developed over the centuries. The story of Robin Hood is a myth which has always been subject to change and adaptation. It still is. The fundamental reason why Robin continues to be part of our culture and other medieval outlaws like Fulk FitzWarin don't is that his legend has always been open to reinterpretation and theirs have not.

This book is an attempt to provide an introduction to Robin Hood in all his incarnations. It begins with two chapters which look at him as he was portrayed in the medieval ballads with which his story began and in the folk-plays of the fifteenth and sixteenth centuries which made him a familiar figure across Tudor England. A third chapter examines the attempts over the years to find a 'real' Robin Hood, an individual from the historical record whose exploits provided the basis for the legend. 'Robin in Literature' and 'Robin on the Screen' provide the heart of the book. Robin's story has become what it is because it has been told and re-told over and over again down the centuries. Different writers and filmmakers have approached it in different ways, adding to it and embellishing it and changing its narrative emphasis. Some of these changes have survived to form part of the familiar tale we all recognise; others have not. These two chapters trace the history of Robin in drama, poetry and fiction and of Robin in the cinema and on TV. Chapters on Robin as he has appeared in illustration and comic books, and in operas and musicals, follow. Two final chapters look at the prospects for Robin's future and at the stories of the other well-known characters in the legend. This is not an academic work and it does not have footnotes but it does end with a list of suggestions for further reading which will provide more information than can be crammed into the pages of a 'Pocket Essential'.

With the exception only of the tales of King Arthur, the story of Robin Hood is the most famous of all England's legends. In many ways, it is the most appealing. It speaks to that part of us which wants to believe that justice and fairness *will* prevail in the face of tyranny. It speaks to that part of us which wants to believe that somewhere there is a place of freedom, a Sherwood Forest, where oppression cannot touch us and we can live better and more honest lives. It is a legend that has survived so long because it has always found ways to change and evolve over the years. Robin Hood has long proved himself an archetypal hero and it seems unlikely that he will die any time soon. This book charts his life so far.

Robin in the Ballads

The very first mention of rhymes of Robin Hood occurs in William Langland's long poem *The Vision of Piers Plowman* which is usually dated to 1377. It is also the very first record of the outlaw hero in literature. In the poem, the character Sloth, who is presented as a drunken and incompetent priest, remarks:

'I kan noght parfitly my Paternoster as the preest it syngeth
But I kan rymes of Robyn Hood and Randolf Erl of Chestre.'

In other words, the negligent Sloth doesn't know the Lord's Prayer, as he should do, but he is familiar with rhymes about Robin Hood and those about a well-known crusading aristocrat from the early thirteenth century. (Clearly stories of Robin were very popular, although the criticism of them continued. Alexander Barclay, in his translation of the German author Sebastian Brant's *The Ship of Fools*, writing more than a century after Langland, sounds a very similar note when he describes those 'so blinded with their foly/That no scriptur think they so true nor gode/As is a foolish jest of Robin Hode'.) What exactly these rhymes were, we cannot be certain. The very first piece of Robin Hood verse to survive is a fragment in a manuscript dating from the early fifteenth century that is now in Lincoln Cathedral. This reads:

'Robin Hood in scherewod stod
Hodud and hathud, hosut and schod
Ffour and thurti arrows he bar in his hondus'

'Robin Hood in Sherwood stood
Hooded and hatted, hosed and shod
Four and thirty arrows he bore in his hands'

Idly scribbled by some anonymous scribe, this may well be the formulaic opening to a Robin Hood poem but nothing more of it exists.

The first ballads that survive in full date from later in the same century. Of these, the longest by far is *A Gest of Robyn Hode* which is first recorded in a printed form in the early 1500s but was certainly written some decades before that. Most scholars today would place its composition in the 1450s or 1460s, although it probably incorporates themes and motifs from earlier, lost works. Consisting of just over 1,800 lines, divided into eight sections known as 'fittes', the poem recounts a series of Robin's adventures which begin when his men bring a melancholy knight to dine with him in the woods. The knight owes money to St. Mary's Abbey in York which he cannot pay and, as a consequence, he is in danger of forfeiting his land and estates to the abbey. Robin takes pity on him and agrees to lend him the money he needs. The knight is able to pay off his debt and thwart the land-grabbing attempts of the greedy clerics. Now all he has to do is save up to pay back Robin. Meanwhile Little John, under the alias of 'Reynolde Grenelef', has joined the service of the 'proude sherif of Notingham' and one day he gets into a fight with the sheriff's cook. After swapping mighty blows, the two men become friends and both decamp from the castle with large amounts of the sheriff's goods and cash. John returns only to tempt the sheriff into the forest where he is ambushed and forced to agree to terms with the outlaws.

Robin is now beginning to wonder about the knight who owes him money. The scheduled day for payment has arrived. Robin sends out his men to look for his debtor but they find only two monks from St. Mary's Abbey. When they lie about the amount of money they are carrying, the outlaws take possession of it and, when the knight does turn up, Robin decides that he has had enough return on his outlay from the monks. He frees the knight of his debt. The enraged sheriff, intent on revenge, later learns of the knight's involvement with the outlaws and takes him prisoner. Robin Hood and his men, outraged by what they see as a breach of the agreement made earlier, go to Nottingham, kill the sheriff and free the knight, now named as Sir Richard at the Lee. The king, who has been told of Robin's exploits, decides to enter the forest disguised as an abbot in an attempt to meet him. As he expects, Robin takes him prisoner and suggests that he should both dine with the outlaws and join with them in their forest sports. When the 'abbot' tells the truth about the amount of money he is carrying with him, Robin takes only half of it. When he bests Robin in one of the games, the outlaw leader recognises the king and agrees to enter his service. He spends a year with the king but the call of the greenwood is too strong and he returns to the forest.

In the last twenty lines of the poem, the author fast-forwards through the years and briefly describes his hero's death, treacherously slain by his kinswoman the Prioress of Kirklee. (A much fuller version of the story of how Robin died is preserved in a ballad entitled 'Robin Hood's Death' which can be found in the seventeenth-century manuscript known as the *Percy Folio*. The manuscript clearly records a tale that is much older and may indeed be one of the oldest of all the Robin Hood stories. The famous episode of Robin shooting an arrow from the window of Kirklees Priory and asking to be buried where it falls is first found in an eighteenth-century broadside version of the ballad. It is probably a later embellishment of the original story, although it may well date back much further than the period in which it is first recorded.)

What then does the *Gest*, the most substantial of all the early Robin Hood texts, tell us about the outlaw hero? He is a yeoman not a nobleman, a fact revealed in the poem's very first stanza. Although some of the action in the *Gest* takes place in Nottingham, Robin comes from Yorkshire not Nottinghamshire. There is no Sherwood in this text. 'Robyn stode in Bernesdale', the poet unequivocally states in the third stanza. The poem opens in Barnsdale in south Yorkshire and this is made abundantly clear by references to other very specific place-names later in the poem. Indeed, the references are so specific and so localised as to suggest that the poet must have had personal knowledge of the area. His chief companions in outlawry are Little John, Much the Miller's Son and 'gode Scarlock' but he has up to 'seven score' of other followers. Robin is a religious man with a particular devotion to the Virgin Mary but he has little or no time for bishops and other members of the higher clergy. The monarch at the time of the action in the *Gest* is not Richard or John but 'Edward, our comly kynge'.

Further information can be gleaned from the handful of shorter ballads which date from much the same period as the *Gest*. 'Robin Hood and the Potter', which survives in a manuscript from about 1500, shows Robin as trickster, disguising himself as a potter to travel into Nottingham and sell his wares. One of his customers is the Sheriff's wife who is so delighted by the bargain she gets on the pots she buys that she invites Robin to dine with her husband. The supposed potter wins an archery contest against the Sheriff's men and, telling his host that he knows the outlaw Robin Hood, he persuades him to travel from the safety of the town into the wilds of the greenwood. There he and his men dispossess the Sheriff of his goods and send him back to Nottingham with his tail between his legs where he faces the scorn and mockery of his wife. 'Robin Hood and Guy of Gisborne' is first found in a seventeenth-century collection but elements in it closely echo a play from 1475 and it must date back to the late fifteenth century. It introduces the character who has, over the centuries, been Robin's most regular opponent other than the Sheriff of Nottingham. This lively and unashamedly violent ballad has Robin and Little John encountering Sir Guy of Gisborne in the 'merry greenwood'. The two outlaws have an argument. John departs to Barnsdale and leaves Robin with Guy who has been hired to kill the outlaw by the Sheriff but does not immediately recognise his prey. He and Robin compete at archery and, when the outlaw wins and identifies himself, they fight to the death. Robin kills his opponent and, cutting off Guy's head, he sticks it 'on his bowes end'. He then takes his 'Irish kniffe' and mutilates the face. Meanwhile Little John has been captured by the Sheriff and faces execution until Robin, now disguised as Guy, approaches and frees his comrade. The Sheriff tries to flee but 'Little John, with an arrow broade/Did cleave his heart in twinn'.

'Robin Hood and the Monk', which can be found in a manuscript at Cambridge University that dates from about 1450, may well be the oldest of all surviving tales of the outlaw. In it, Robin, anxious to attend mass, travels to Nottingham where a 'gret-hedid munke' (a large-headed monk) recognises him and tells the Sheriff of his presence in the town. The outlaw is captured. Little John and Much the Miller's Son, when they learn what has happened, determine to rescue their master. They encounter the monk and his page. John kills the monk (he 'smote of the munkis hed') and Much does the same to the page for fear the boy would be a witness against them. They take letters from the monk and deliver them to the king who accepts their story that the monk died a natural death. The king now charges John and Much with the task of travelling to Nottingham to bring Robin to him. With the king's blessing they have little trouble in getting into the prison where their leader is being held. They kill the jailer and free Robin.

Even the briefest summaries of 'Robin Hood and Guy of Gisborne' and 'Robin Hood and the Monk' reveal an important fact about these early ballads. One of the most striking elements in them is their casual violence. Although Robin and his followers are capable of courtesy and generosity, and they have, in their own way, a rather strict code of justice and morality, they are also men with no qualms about killing their enemies and mutilating their bodies after doing so. As the historian Maurice Keen has written, 'In the ballads, we are up against a full-blooded medieval brigand.' Nor were the men who created the ballads particularly troubled by this. The violence is described in very much the same casual, off-handed way in which it is committed.

Other old ballads about Robin exist – close to thirty of them – but none has the same age and provenance as the *Gest* and the handful of other, shorter works just described. Many of them undoubtedly incorporate early material but it is impossible to trace it back to its original sources. The ballads which survive from the seventeenth century do so in a variety of forms. Some are found in manuscripts. The so-called *Percy Folio*, a huge compilation of old ballads and poetry of all kinds, is written in a seventeenth-century hand but has material in it that dates back centuries before that. It contains first surviving texts of some of the best-known Robin ballads including 'Robin Hood and the Curtal Friar', an introduction to the character later known as Friar Tuck, and 'Robin Hood Rescuing Will Stutly'. Some appeared as broadsides, printed on a single sheet of paper and sold in the city streets and at markets and fairs. Some were produced as chapbooks, pocket-sized booklets designed to be sold by the travelling pedlars known as chapmen. Over the years they were accumulated by collectors intrigued by these examples of popular culture (the diarist Samuel

Pepys was one avid enthusiast) or they were gathered together in what were known as 'garlands', short anthologies of ballads from different sources. The first major, scholarly attempt to bring all the known ballads together in one book was made by a man named Joseph Ritson in 1795.

Some of these later ballads probably date back in their entirety far further than their first appearance in print or preserved manuscript. Others re-work or make use of themes and motifs from the earlier ballads. As on an archaeological site, a little digging can soon unearth elements of older structures. Look beneath the surface of 'Robin Hood and the Butcher', a ballad which first survives in the seventeenth-century *Percy Folio*, and it is clear that it is derived from 'Robin Hood and the Potter', a ballad which may well date back to the 1460s. In both works, Robin is the trickster figure, who takes possession of a tradesman's wares (the potter's pots, the butcher's meat) and sells them at ridiculously low prices. In both, he first feasts with the Sheriff and then fools him into accompanying him back to Sherwood. There the representative of the law is captured when Robin summons his men. He is only released because of the hospitality his wife had extended to the outlaw when he was disguised as a tradesman.

The stories told in the other ballads are various and wide-ranging. Some, such as the tale of 'Robin Hood and the Curtal Friar', have become part of the tradition and have appeared under assorted guises in dozens of books and films; others have failed to catch readers' imaginations and have never been repeated in later works. A few stray (usually unsuccessfully) from the standard territory of Barnsdale and Sherwood. In 'Robin Hood and the Prince of Aragon', for example, the outlaw leader, together with Little John and Will Scadlock, travels to London where the eponymous prince is besieging the city with the help of two giants. There Robin and his men take on the three villains of the piece and slay them in combat. Elements of more fantastical romances are uneasily welded to the down-to-earth tradition of the Robin Hood myth. In 'Robin Hood's Fishing', the setting is once again an unusual one but this ballad retains some of the feel of those which take place on more familiar ground. Self-confessedly 'weary of the woods' and the 'chasing of the fallow deer', Robin decides to leave them and set up as a fisherman in Scarborough. He proves useless at his new trade but, when the fishing vessels are raided by French pirates, he comes into his own. Bound to the main mast so he can aim properly amidst the rolling of the sea, Robin despatches Frenchman after Frenchman with his bow and eventually the fishermen board the pirate ship and take possession of 'twelve hundred pounds in gold so bright'.

There are recurring themes and motifs in these ballads. Robin regularly comes across some traveller in the forest and, almost invariably, he offers to fight with him. This happens in 'Robin Hood and the Ranger', 'Robin Hood and the Shepherd', 'Robin Hood and the Tinker' and several more. Almost invariably, Robin is beaten. The outlaw hero then invites the man who has bested him to join the band of merry men. Nearly anyone who has seen a Robin Hood film in the past seventy years has seen a version of this 'Robin Meets His Match' encounter but all the versions ultimately derive from the ballads. However, it is not just strangers who end up quarrelling in the greenwood. In the ballads, the outlaws themselves are always falling out with one another. Robin and Little John are forever setting off on journeys through the woods, having words and going their separate ways to meet with separate adventures.

Disguise and the adoption of another's identity also have significant roles to play in many of the ballads. Robin frequently appears as a trickster figure who disguises himself to fool or undermine authority, usually in the shape of the Sheriff of Nottingham. As we have seen, this occurs in the earliest of the stories such as 'Robin Hood and the Potter' but it is also an element in many of the later ones as well. In 'Robin Hood Rescues Three Young Men', for example, the outlaw pretends to be the hangman in order to thwart the Sheriff's plan to hang 'three squires in Nottingham town' who have committed no crime other than the killing of the king's deer. Finally, the forest itself is of huge importance to the Robin Hood ballads. As a place where the normal rules of society do not apply and where the social hierarchy can so easily be overturned, Sherwood (or Barnsdale) is a realm of new possibilities for those who, like Robin, choose to live in it.

For anyone familiar with Robin Hood largely through movies and TV, or even through any one of the dozens of children's books based on the character that have appeared in the last hundred years, the outlaw of the ballads can come as a bit of a surprise. He isn't a gentleman fallen on hard times, forced into the greenwood by his loyalty to Richard the Lionheart, nor has he ever fought with the king in the Crusades. He doesn't even live in the time of Richard the Lionheart. The king in the ballads, if he is mentioned at all, is called Edward. Robin is happy enough to rob the rich but he doesn't appear to have any particular desire to hand over his spoils to the poor. (Although the *Gest* shows his generosity to the poor knight Sir Richard at the Lee and ends with lines assuring readers that he 'dyde pore men moch god [good]'.) He's actually a violent and aggressive man who has no qualms about mutilating a dead man's face with his knife. The goodies in the stories aren't stalwart Saxons and the baddies nasty Normans. There is no hint whatsoever of any ethnic struggle between Saxons and Normans. Except in one later ballad that may have been deliberately written to add an element to the tradition that wasn't previously there, Robin doesn't have a Sherwood romance with a lovely lady known as Maid Marian. In fact, he rarely has any lovely lady friend at all.

And yet these early ballads do contain familiar foundations of the Robin Hood story on which later generations have built ever more elaborate narrative structures. Robin's principal friends and allies (Little John, Will Scarlet, Much the Miller's Son) are all to be found in them. So too are the villains and enemies associated with Robin, most notably the Sheriff of Nottingham and Sir Guy of Gisbourne. The location in many of the ballads is Nottingham and/or Sherwood Forest, although a handful of them, particularly the earliest, mention Barnsdale and other Yorkshire place names. There are themes and motifs in the ballads – Robin meeting his match, Robin playing the trickster, Robin being rescued from imprisonment or rescuing others from imprisonment – that would be immediately recognised by fans of, say, the recent BBC TV series about the outlaw leader. Look again at *A Gest of Robyn Hode*, by far the longest and possibly the oldest of all the Robin Hood ballads that we have. There are elements in its narrative that have lasted throughout the centuries. The archery contest appears in various guises in works as different as *Ivanhoe*, Sir Walter Scott's novel of 1819, and Disney's 1973 animated feature film entitled *Robin Hood*. The story of the impoverished knight Sir Richard at the Lee and his debt to the Abbey of St. Mary's is still being re-enacted 500 years later in episodes of the 1950s TV series starring Richard Greene. Robin of the ballads is still with us.

Robin in the May Games

The ballads played a central role in keeping alive the stories of Robin Hood for hundreds of years, from the time of Langland to the time of Sir Walter Scott, but there is a good argument to be made that, for at least two of those centuries, Robin Hood was best-known throughout England in the plays, games, revels and pageants which featured him as a character. For various reasons, Robin became a central figure in the tradition of folk-drama that was particularly associated with the May Games played throughout the country at Whitsuntide. Like Morris men and the summer lord, he was part of the ritualistic fabric of the English year. The very first reference to Robin which relates to these games dates to 1427, at least twenty years before the earliest possible date for any of the surviving ballads. In the municipal records for the city of Exeter for that year, there is an entry detailing the 20d that was paid *lusoribus ludentibus lusum Robyn Hode*, in other words 'for the players playing the game of Robin Hood'. For the next two hundred years, these players seem to have been familiar figures in communities throughout southern England, the south Midlands and Scotland. (Curiously, almost no evidence survives for them from the very areas – the north and the north midlands – where the Robin Hood stories are set. Nor is there much recorded activity in East Anglia apart from one major reference discussed below.) There are more than a hundred surviving records in parish accounts and the like of instances of these Robin Hood games. In Bristol in 1525, we hear of the purchase of 'two pair of hosyn for Robin Hood and Lytyll John'; in 1536, a parish in Cornwall receives a sum of money from 'John Marys and his company that playd Robin Hoode'; in Yeovil between the 1510s and 1570s there are more than twenty records of both outgoings (for such things as the refeathering of Robin Hood's arrows and ribbon lace for Little John's horn) and the receipt of charitable donations; in Leicester in 1526 there is a reference to money owed to St. Leonard's Church after a Robin Hood play was acted for its benefit; and eight years earlier and much further north, in Edinburgh, a man is told in a letter that 'Francis Boithwell your nichtbour is chosin to be Litiljohn for to mak sportis and jocositeis in the toun'.

These were clearly regular and familiar events through large swathes of the country and Robin Hood was not just popular with ordinary villagers and townsfolk. He was also popular amongst the gentry. The Paston Letters is the name generally given to a large collection of family letters and papers connected to the Pastons of East Anglia, a family rising up the social ladder in the fifteenth century, the period covered in the correspondence. Amongst the Paston Letters is one from 1473 in which Sir John Paston, then head of the family, refers to a servant whom he has kept for three years 'to pleye Seynt Jorge and Robynhod and the shryff off Notyngham'. The man has now left his employ and Sir John is not best pleased about his departure. Clearly Paston was accustomed to stage Robin Hood plays (and plays involving St. George) in his own household and this particular servant, named as W. Woode and presumably a particularly effective actor, will be missed when they are next performed.

The very play in which W. Woode might well have acted has survived in fragmentary form in a manuscript, now in the library of Trinity College, which, in all likelihood, was once part of an archive of Paston family documents. Usually known as 'Robyn Hod and the Shryff of Nottingham', the drama consists of a mere 21 lines.

In the original manuscript there is no division into scenes or any indication of which characters speak which lines but a narrative of sorts can be extrapolated from what we have. It has clear similarities to the ballad 'Robin Hood and Guy of Gisborne'. In a first scene, a knight is commissioned by the Sheriff to capture Robin. The unnamed knight and the outlaw meet and compete against one another in various activities including archery and wrestling. The two then fight with swords and Robin wins, cutting off his opponent's head. In a second scene, Robin and some of his men have been captured and the other outlaws, including Friar Tuck (appearing in the literature for the first time), must effect their rescue. It's a lot to fit into 21 lines and it is clear that these Robin Hood folk dramas depended for their impact not on the spoken word but on boisterous action and plenty of it. Other texts of May Games plays have survived. One of the sixteenth-century printings of the *Gest* also includes two short dramatic texts which, according to the man who printed them, 'are very proper to be played in Maye Games'. The first depicts Robin's initial meeting with Friar Tuck, a story also told in a ballad entitled 'Robin Hood and the Curtal Friar'. However, the play text pre-dates the first surviving version of the ballad by a century. The second text shares some of the elements of the ballad 'Robin Hood and the Potter' and is a version of the story, re-told many times and with many variations, in which Robin meets his match in a fight with a stranger in the greenwood. Although these are longer by far than 'Robyn Hod and the Shryff of Nottingham' (together they amount to just over 200 lines), they also clearly indicate that the dramas in the May Games depended far more on action than they did on words.

At the height of the popularity of the May Games, even the king might play at Robin Hood. The royal court, just as much as the village green or the city street, could be the setting for such revels. In Edward Hall's *Chronicle* there is an account of Henry VIII and his courtiers imitating the pursuits of lesser folk by indulging in Robin Hood games. On May Day in 1510, according to Hall, Henry, together with the earls of Essex and Wiltshire and other noblemen, burst into the Queen's chamber, 'all appareled in short cotes of Kentish Kendal, with hodes on their heddes, and hosen of the same, everyone of them with his bowe and arrowes, and a sworde and buckler, like outlawes, or Robyn Hodes men.'

What was the purpose of these games when they were played not by king and courtiers but by ordinary townsfolk and villagers? Despite the fact that Robin was an anti-authority figure, metaphorically sticking up two fingers to the forces of law and the higher echelons of the church, there is no indication that they represented popular resistance to authority. They sometimes ended in riots and violence, amidst all the drink and excitement that accompanied them, but they were not intended to trouble the social order. In fact, they were usually organised by village or town officials and substantial amounts of public money were lavished on them. Surviving records from Kingston upon Thames show just how much was spent on ensuring that the players were well-costumed. In 1508, the sizeable sum of 12s 10d was forked out for Kendal green cloth to make coats for the two men taking the roles of Robin and Little John. Ten years later, Robin's retinue had clearly increased and the old coats had grown threadbare. Another fourteen were commissioned to replace them.

Yet the Kingston authorities and others like them, through their generosity, were speculating in the hope of accumulating. For the prime purpose of the Robin Hood play-games seems to have been fundraising. In the course of the day's entertainment, Robin and Little John, Friar Tuck and Maid Marian (often played by a man in drag) processed through town or village, stopping from time to time to perform their mini-dramas but devoting much of their energies to the gathering of money from fellow citizens. Robin was not taking from the rich to give to the poor but from the individual to give to the community. Most often the money went to the churchwardens to be devoted to communal projects. In Croscombe in Somerset, there are records from the 1480s to the 1510s of sums ranging from 23s 8d to £3 6s 8d received as 'Roben Hode money' or as a result of 'the sport of Robart Hode and hys company' or designated as coming, in some way, from the Robin Hood games in May. In Yeovil in 1544, £5 8s 9½d was received from 'John Delagryse being R Hood this yere'. Further north in Melton Mowbray, Leicestershire in 1556, townwardens' accounts include 29s 8d gathered by a man named Steven Shaw and his company for their 'Robyn Hood playe' performed for the last two years. And, in Kingston itself, outlay on costumes was more than justified by the returns recorded by the churchwardens. From 1506 to the late 1530s sums ranging from 12s up to £5 6s 8d are described in the accounts as received for 'ye gaderyng of Robyn Hode' or in similar words.

Despite the connection with charitable gathering and good works, church disapproval of Robin Hood and the May Games was growing by the middle decades of the sixteenth century. In increasingly Protestant times, these popular rituals and sports smacked too much of Catholic laxity and the papist past. In a sermon delivered before Edward VI in 1549, Bishop Hugh Latimer recalled an incident years previously in which his own attempts to preach in a church he was visiting had been thwarted by popular enthusiasm for the outlaw. 'Sir, this is a busy day with us, we cannot hear you,' one of the parishioners had told him, 'it is Robin Hood's day. The parish are gone abroad to gather for Robin Hood.' More than a decade later the bishop was still fuming. 'It is no laughing matter, my friends,' he thundered, perhaps suspecting that some people would indeed find it a laughing matter, 'it is a weeping matter, a heavy matter; a heavy matter, under the pretence of gathering for Robin Hood, a traitor and a thief, to put out a preacher, to have his office less esteemed; to prefer Robin

Hood before the ministration of God's word.' Attempts were made to repress Robin Hood activities in the May Games. In 1528, the Lord Warden of the Cinque Ports issued an edict banning Robin Hood games in the towns he controlled; nearly thirty years later and several hundred miles further north, the Scottish parliament even went so far as to pass a statute to prevent people from performing the plays. It failed to work. In 1561, the fearsome kirk leader John Knox noted that people were still gathering in Edinburgh 'efter the auld wikket manner of Robyn Hoode' and that, although the practice had been condemned, 'yet would they not be forbidden, but would disobey and trouble the town'. The trouble ended in a riot when one of the Robin Hood revellers was arrested and his fellows descended on the Tolbooth to free him.

And yet, despite the disapproval of the authorities, the old traditions were still much in evidence. The Tudor diarist Henry Machyn, a clothier in London, refers to May Games in the capital in 1559 which included 'Robyn Hode and Lytyll John... and Frere Tuke' alongside 'Sant Gorge and the Dragon' and 'the mores dansse'. Outside the capital, records of Robin Hood continue to be found. In Barnstaple in Devon, in the same year that Machyn was watching May Games, 3s 4d was 'paid to Robart Hode for his pastime' and the Yeovil records mention Robin well into the 1570s. In Kent in 1574, younger members of the aristocratic Sidney family were charitably doling out cash to players performing in Robin Hood plays. It is only with the general decline of such rituals and folk dramas in the last decades of the sixteenth century that Robin Hood play-games finally begin to disappear from the records. Even then, in remoter and more conservative regions such as Cornwall, Robin of the May Games could still flourish. There are records of Robin Hood costumes in the town of St. Columb Major in 1588 and of the gathering of 'Robin hoodes monyes' six years later. By the beginning of the seventeenth century, the assumption may be that such age-old sports were finally gone but the odd reference suggests that there were pockets of the country where Robin still held sway from time to time. He is mentioned in a processional May-game in Wells in 1607 and, in Woodstock in Oxfordshire in 1627, there is a record of £7 7s 1d brought in by Robin Hood and Little John which sounds little different to entries in parish accounts from a hundred years earlier. The most surprising record, and the one most difficult to explain, dates from as late as 1652. In that year, villagers in Enstone in Oxfordshire were, according to the Latin account of two foreign visitors, still celebrating games 'quos sua lingua Rabben Hut vocabant' ('which in their own language, they call Rabben Hut'). Three years after the execution of Charles I, with England under the rule of the Commonwealth, Robin was somehow surviving as a character in folk drama. Perhaps, in a sense, the Robin Hood plays never died. They merely went into hibernation, awaiting the revival of interest in such folk traditions in the twentieth century.

Historical Robin

Was Robin Hood a real person? Or was he, as the historian JC Holt claims, 'a legend rather than a man'? If he was a real individual, is there any trace of him in the historical record? In a sense, the questions are superfluous. It is Robin Hood the living mythic figure who holds our attention not some long-dead medieval outlaw who may have been known by that name or a similar one. And yet the question of whether or not Robin Hood really existed is one that will not go away. Historians and pseudo-historians have been striving to answer it for centuries. One of the most distinguished scholars who ever studied the Robin Hood ballads, the American Francis J. Child, was of the opinion that anyone who made a connection between any ballad and a specific historical record must be possessed of 'an uncommon insensibility to the ludicrous' but there have been plenty of people over the years prepared to risk looking silly in the pursuit of a real Robin.

Certainly there were plenty of real-life gangs of outlaws in the Middle Ages. Eustace Folville and his younger brothers, for example, delinquent members of a gentry family, led a band of thieves and thugs who committed a series of often violent crimes in Leicestershire and Derbyshire in the 1320s and 1330s. Summoned for trial in 1326 for the murder of a local knight, the Folvilles simply headed for the hills and were declared outlaws. Over the next decade, they were responsible for most of the worst law-breaking in the Midlands. Eustace himself is mentioned in the records in connection with three robberies and four murders in the space of a few years. Despite this, there was clearly a good deal of sympathy for the Folvilles amongst ordinary people and a sense that these outlaws were more honest men than the officers of the law who pursued them. Rendered into modern English, the complaint of one official was that the Folvilles 'are aided and abetted by local people, who incite them to their evil deeds and shield them after they are done'. He could have been talking about Robin and his merry men. Thirty years after his death, Eustace Folville was still remembered as a fundamentally just man. In 1377, William Langland wrote approvingly in *Piers Plowman*, the poem in which the first mention of Robin Hood literature is made, of 'Folvyles lawes', the rough and ready justice that the brothers had embodied.

The Folvilles made no mark on literature beyond this passing reference in *Piers Plowman* but there were also real outlaws from earlier times whose lives were recorded in verse and prose. Hereward the Wake was a hero of the Saxon resistance to the Norman Conquest who defied the Conqueror's men from his stronghold on the isle of Ely. Tales of his exploits survive in a number of medieval works, most notably *Gesta Herewardi* ('The Deeds of Hereward'), the earliest copy of which dates from the middle of the thirteenth century. Fulk FitzWarin was a nobleman turned outlaw, a landowner from the Welsh Marches who rebelled against King John in the first decade of the twelfth century. His adventures are recorded in a prose romance in Old French entitled *Fouk le Fitz Waryn* which survives in a compilation of works written by a scribe in Hereford sometime between 1325 and 1340. Eustace the Monk was a Benedictine who left his monastery in about 1190 and went on to become an outlaw and pirate. He was killed in the naval Battle of Dover in 1217. Some time in the decades immediately following his death, he became the subject of *Wistasse li Moine*, a French poem which focuses particularly on his early career as a forest outlaw, fighting and feuding with his former lord, the count of Boulogne. All of these outlaws were undoubtedly real, historical figures and the works of literature which were written about them carry unmistakeable echoes of the earliest stories of the most famous outlaw leader of them all. Clearly elements of the stories of Hereward, Fulk and Eustace found their way into the Robin Hood tradition. This does not necessarily prove that Robin, like them, was a real individual.

To some writers, beginning in the nineteenth century, Robin was most definitely not a real man but a figure from ancient mythology, one 'whose name but faintly disguises either Woden in the aspect of a vegetation deity, or a minor wood spirit Hode'. In the twentieth century, folklorists such as Margaret Murray saw him as a high priest of the ancient pagan religion, representative of the horned god of nature. Such theories, although they have been regularly revealed as based more on wishful thinking than any real evidence, refuse to go away. In the 1990s, John Matthews, a prolific explorer of the territory where mythology and new age spirituality meet, published *Robin Hood: The Green Lord of the Wildwood* in which he reaffirmed links between the outlaw leader and the ancient symbol of the Green Man which had been largely discredited decades earlier. Discarding such outré ideas may be essential in any pursuit of the real Robin Hood but it still does not necessarily involve the belief that the hero of the greenwood can be traced back to a specific individual from the Middle Ages.

So where should we look if we are in pursuit of a real Robin? It would seem as if place names that indicate a connection with the outlaw (Robin Hood's Bay on the Yorkshire coast, Robin Hood's Close in Nottingham, Robin Hood's Cave in the Creswell Crags between Nottinghamshire and Derbyshire) might provide some clues. However, the dates when these place names are first recorded reveal that they almost certainly reflect the widespread popularity of the stories in song and folklore rather than any link to a real person named Robin Hood.

What about the names of individuals most commonly associated with him in the popular imagination? Most of these can also be swiftly dismissed in the search. Despite what some twentieth-century filmmakers and TV scriptwriters would have us believe, he was not Robert, Earl of Huntington. Robin makes his earliest appearances in the ballads as a yeoman not a noble and it seems that the first person to identify him as the Earl of Huntington was the Elizabethan dramatist Anthony Munday in two plays from the 1590s.

Nor was the outlaw's real name Robert of Locksley, Robin of Loxley or any of the other similar variants that have been used in dozens of books and films in the years since Walter Scott introduced his Robin Hood character as 'Locksley' in his 1819 novel *Ivanhoe*. It is true that a manuscript which forms part of the Sloane Collection in the British Museum, probably written in the late sixteenth century, is the first surviving attempt to provide a historical biography of Robin Hood and that this places him in the time of Richard I and records his birthplace as Locksley. However, there is no evidence that the writer of the 'Sloane Life' had access to records that have now been lost. Most of the rest of his biography is quite clearly constructed from material in the ballads. The Locksley birthplace is surely more likely to have come from a lost ballad than from lost historical evidence. There are other early references to Locksley as Robin's name. Roger Dodsworth, for instance, a seventeenth-century antiquarian, wrote: 'Robert Locksley, born in Bradfield parish, in Hallamshire, wounded his stepfather to death at plough: fled into the woods, and was relieved by his mother till he was discovered. Then he came to Clifton upon Calder, and came acquainted with Little John, that kept the kine which said John is buried at Hathershead

(Hathersage) in Derbyshire, where he hath a fair tomb-stone with an inscription.' Yet, since Dodsworth also goes on to refer to the possibility that it was Little John who was the Earl of Huntington, it doesn't seem as if a great deal of credence can be placed on his theories.

In looking for a real Robin, the first references to him as an historical figure rather than a literary one are significant. They come, perhaps surprisingly, from Scotland. Two fifteenth-century Scottish chroniclers, both of them churchmen, record the outlaw's activities in their works. Andrew of Wyntoun, writing about 1420, places Robin in the year 1283. In an entry for that year in his *Orygynale Chronicle*, Andrew writes: 'Litil Iohun and Robert Hude/Waythmen war commendit gud/In Ingilwode and Bernnysdaile/Thai oyssit al this tyme thar trawale'. ('Little John and Robert Hood were forest outlaws who were highly praised. In Inglewood and Barnsdale, they undertook their labour all this time.') Some twenty years later Walter Bower, writing in Latin, placed Robin in the 1260s, casting him as one of the followers of Simon de Montfort, Earl of Leicester, forced into banditry after the defeat and death of the Earl at the Battle of Evesham in 1265 – 'Then arose the famous murderer (*siccarius*, literally 'cut-throat') Robert Hood, as well as Little John, together with their accomplices from among the disinherited, whom the foolish populace are so inordinately fond of celebrating both in tragedies and comedies, and about whom they are delighted to hear the jesters and minstrels sing above all other ballads.' It is worth noting that neither Andrew of Wyntoun nor Walter Bower mentions Nottinghamshire. Andrew places him in Barnsdale in Yorkshire and further north in Inglewood, probably an area near Carlisle. And neither of them puts Robin in the period with which later generations have come to associate him – the reign of Richard I – but nearly a hundred years later.

The first historian to associate the outlaw with Richard the Lionheart was another Scotsman named John Major, author of a *History of Great Britain*, originally written in Latin, and published in 1521. Major also played a significant role in the process of transforming Robin from yeoman outlaw to a man of gentility and humanity. 'Robert Hood, an Englishman, and Little John,' he wrote, not only 'lay in wait in the woods' but they also 'spoiled of their goods those only that were wealthy'. These were not just bloody cutthroats. 'They took the life of no man, unless he either attacked them or offered resistance in defence of his property.' Robin was basically, in Major's eyes, a decent chap. 'He would allow no woman to suffer injustice, nor would he spoil the poor, but rather enriched them from the plunder taken from the abbots.' In short, Robin Hood was – there was no getting away from it – a robber but 'of all robbers he was the humanest and the chief'.

As the sixteenth century progressed, other antiquarians, including famous names like John Leland, sometimes called 'the father of English local history', and John Stow, the author of *A Survey of London*, tended to repeat what Major had said and the association of Robin with the reigns of Richard I and John began to gather strength. For close to two hundred years there were few significant developments in the story of the search for an historical Robin. As we have seen, a prose life of the outlaw, dating from about 1600, was preserved in the Sloane Manuscripts but it is merely constructed from ballads, folk plays and tradition. Even four centuries ago, it seems that there was little hard historical evidence to hand. One of the traditions that existed was that Robin Hood's Grave could be seen in Kirklees in Yorkshire where there was certainly a stone that was linked to the outlaw. It was described by the antiquarian William Camden in 1607 and drawn by a local doctor named Nathaniel Johnston sixty years later. Forty years after

Johnston, the Dean of York, Thomas Gale, not only recorded a date for Robin's death which he claimed was on the grave (the improbable 24 Kalends of December 1247) but also some lines from a verse epitaph. 'Hear underneath this laitl stean/Laid Robert earl of Huntington/Nea arcir vir as hei sae geud/An pipl kauld im robin heud.' Presumably this was some kind of clerical joke since this gibberish bears no relation to any form of Middle English and the scholarly Gale must have known this. He seems to have taken the verse from Martin Parker's *A True Tale of Robin Hood* from 1632 and turned it into cod medieval English for fun. The joke took on a life of its own when, sometime in the eighteenth century, the words were carved onto another stone slab near Kirklees which is still there.

Probably not intended as a joke but no less ludicrous than Gale's epitaph was the family tree constructed for Robin Hood by the eccentric antiquarian William Stukeley. In 1746, Stukeley took the genuine pedigree of a series of medieval earls of Huntington and inserted into it some names which, as far as one can tell, he had simply made up. He invented a family of Fitzooths and proudly stated at the bottom of this false pedigree that one of them, Robert Fitzooth, was 'commonly called Robin Hood' and was the 'pretended earl of Huntington'. Quite what Stukeley's motives were in creating Robin's family tree are unclear but he had a track record in holding barmy ideas about the past. He was genuinely a major figure in the history of the development of British archaeology and one of the first people to investigate Stonehenge in anything approaching a scientific fashion but he was also the proponent of some markedly offbeat theories. His local patriotism was such that he decided that Stamford in Lincolnshire, the county of his birth, was a seat of learning far older than Oxford and Cambridge. In fact, he argued there had been a university there in the ninth century BC, founded by Bladud, the legendary king of Britain who also established the city of Bath. One of his contemporaries described Stukeley as a mixture of 'simplicity, drollery, absurdity, ingenuity, superstition and antiquarianism' and the kindest assumption about his ideas on Robin Hood's ancestry is that, in constructing the family tree, he demonstrated his simplicity and superstition rather more than he did his ingenuity and antiquarianism.

Not much reliance should have been placed on Stukeley's 'researches' at all but, alas, people continued to do so for decades after his death. (Some people even do so today.) In 1864, an antiquarian and prolific dramatist named JR Planché published a paper entitled 'A Ramble with Robin Hood' in which he argued that Stukeley had got the name 'Fitzooth' wrong and that it should have been 'Fitzodo'. There was a Fitzodo family in records from the late twelfth century which traced its descent from Bishop Odo, William the Conqueror's half-brother and a man who had paid little attention to any notions of priestly chastity. Planché speculated that the 'Fitz', which implied illegitimacy, had been dropped from the name and that some members of the family had called themselves simply 'Odo' or 'Ode'. He even found a Robert Fitzodo in the 1190s who could have been 'Robert Ode' or Robin Hood. In truth, of course, Planché was barking up the wrong tree by paying any attention whatsoever to Stukeley's absurd pedigree but he must have been further excited because the Fitzodos at the time were lords of the manor of Loxley, a village in Warwickshire.

So far we have only considered the slow development of past ideas about Robin's historical reality and the names of those proposed can be readily dismissed. What about candidates for the 'real' Robin Hood whose case can still be argued? One of the strongest of these was first put forward in 1852, twelve years before Planché went off on his rambles with 'Robert Ode'. Joseph Hunter was a Yorkshireman who became an assistant keeper at the Public Record Office. Fascinated by the old ballads of Robin

Hood, he decided to see whether or not there was anything in the medieval records which supported the story told in the *Gest*. He noted that the king in the *Gest* is named as 'Edwarde, our comly kynge' and that this king is on a progress through the north during events described in the poem. Hunter decided that the only king this could be was Edward II who was indeed journeying through the north of England between April and November of 1323. Furthermore, the following year, a Robert or Robyn Hood appears in the service of Edward II. Perhaps, Hunter thought, this man could be the same Robert Hode who appears in the Court Rolls of Wakefield, close to Barnsdale, in 1316 and 1317. He constructed a plausible enough story to fit his man with some of the narrative supplied in the *Gest*. So far Hunter was on relatively firm evidential ground but he went on, rather more shakily, to argue that the man must have been a supporter of the uprising by Thomas, Earl of Lancaster against Edward II and that he had become an outlaw after Lancaster's rebels had been defeated at the Battle of Boroughbridge in 1322. The records are those of a man who has returned to the king's favour after a period of exile. Although there are huge gaps in the evidence Hunter used, his theory does have points in its favour and it has been revisited several times since he first proposed it. It has, for instance, been repeated, as if it was an astonishing revelation, in the 1995 book *Robin Hood: The Man Behind the Myth* by Graham Phillips and Martin Keatman.

Since Hunter first ventured into the medieval records in search of a man called Hood, many others have followed in his wake and many other potential Robins have emerged. Some date back much further than Robert Hood of Wakefield and there is a good argument that the earlier the Hood the more likely he is to be the right man. The first mention of Robin Hood rhymes dates from the 1370s, only half a century after Hunter's Hood was alive. Go back a bit further and there is more time for the legend to have developed. One of the most promising of all candidates for the real 'Robin' dates back a century before Robert Hood of Wakefield. He was first put forward by a local historian named LVD Owen in 1936 who found him in the records of York Assizes for 1225–26. They refer to a 'Robert Hod' who is described as a 'fugitivus' and state that the chattels left behind by this man were worth 32s 6d. The same name (or variants of it such as 'Robert Hood' and 'Hobbehod') appears in later entries in the same records and can be safely assumed to refer to the same man. He is the only man found in the records with the right name who was almost certainly an outlaw. It is difficult to see what else the word 'fugitivus' could mean other than that he was on the run from the law.

However, this Yorkshire fugitive is only one of a number of men with the name of 'Robert Hod' or something very similar that diligent researchers have unearthed in medieval records. There is a 'Robert Hod' who was a servant of a Gloucestershire abbot. He was in trouble in the reign of King John after killing one Ralf of Cirencester. Another 'Robert Hod' was among rebels supporting Simon de Montfort who took refuge on the Isle of Ely in the 1260s. Two more Yorkshire Robert Hods fell foul of the law, one in the 1250s and one in the following decade. Move on to the fourteenth century and there is a 'Robyn Hod' serving as an archer in a garrison on the Isle of Wight and yet another 'Robert Hod' who was imprisoned for stealing venison in the Forest of Rockingham in Northamptonshire in 1354. There are strong arguments against particular Robert Hods being the original of the legendary Robin Hood. The Rockingham thief, for example, is far too close in date to the first mention of Robin Hood ballads in *Piers Plowman* in 1377 for there to have been time for the ballad stories to develop. The Gloucestershire murderer is too geographically distant from the familiar settings of Sherwood and Barnsdale to make him a likely candidate. However, there is a general argument against all of them in that, because of the limited nature of the records, there is no evidence to link any of them with the activities ascribed to Robin Hood in the earliest stories. Even Robert Hod/Hobbehod from the 1220s, who is specifically described as a 'fugitive' and who might seem the best of these candidates, cannot be directly connected with the traditional Robin. The evidence is simply not there and it is never likely to be.

This has not stopped writers regularly stepping forward with new theories about Robin Hood's identity. Nottingham author Jim Lees has suggested that Robert de Kyme, the eldest son of a minor lord named William de Kyme, who was outlawed for robbery in the 1220s had a career that paralleled some of the events in the *Gest*. Unfortunately, Lees's ideas are severely compromised by his continued reliance, to some extent, on the long-discredited pedigree produced by William Stukeley in the 1740s. Lees believes that Stukeley was on to something; most Robin Hood scholars very definitely do not. Another author from the area most associated with the outlaw, Tony Molyneux-Smith, has come up with a theory that Robin Hood was not an individual but a pseudonym adopted by successive generations of the Foliot family from north Nottinghamshire. His book, *Robin Hood and the Lords of Wellow*, is a short and intriguing read but falls a long way short of proving his case.

Yet a further candidate who has come to the fore in recent years is Roger Godberd. Godberd was undoubtedly a medieval outlaw, a man who had served under Simon de Montfort at the Battle of Evesham in 1265 and suffered as a consequence of being on the losing side. He also had connections with Nottingham and Sherwood Forest. As David Baldwin, Godberd's most persuasive advocate, writes in his 2010 book *Robin Hood: The English Outlaw Unmasked*, there are certainly 'several quite striking parallels between what is known of Roger Godberd's deeds and the earliest ballads'. One of the strengths of Baldwin's argument is that he makes no outrageous claims on its behalf. He does not state definitively that Godberd is the one and only real Robin. 'The character of Robin Hood,' he admits, 'has drawn on many sources over the centuries (and continues to do so)' but, he continues, 'there are enough similarities to conclude that Roger's career lies at the heart of it.'

There has even been a recent theory that Robin was a Templar. Some unkind souls, when hearing of this, might be reminded of the quote from Umberto Eco's *Foucault's Pendulum* which states that a lunatic can always be identified, among other ways, 'by the fact that sooner or later he brings up the Templars' but, in fact, the case for Robin the Templar is not an unreasonable one. The argument, put forward in books like John Paul Davis's *Robin Hood: The Unknown Templar* is that Robin and his men, in the ballads, show many characteristics which suggest they are Templars escaped to the safety of the greenwood after the often violent dissolution of the order in the first two decades of the fourteenth century. Like members of a Christian military religious order, the Merry Men combine piety with martial skills. They obey one master, Robin Hood, and the ballads indicate that most of them were outlawed together. None appears to be married and indeed women seem to play no part in their lives. Their robberies are designed not to profit themselves as individuals but to contribute to a common fund. They show kindness to one another and to the poor but something approaching contempt for government officials and the richer members of the Church. Superficially the argument is quite appealing but it founders again on the rocky fact that there is no hard documentary evidence for a link between the theory and any of the early stories of Robin Hood. In the unavoidable absence of this, all is speculation. To some, it may seem highly plausible speculation; to others, it is much less so. But it remains speculation. So do all the attempts to identify a real man behind the mask of Robin Hood. The mythical Robin, the Robin of books and films and computer games, lives on and shows few signs of ever dying. The real Robin, if he ever existed, has been sadly lost to history and there is very little likelihood that he will ever be rescued from time's oblivion.

Robin in Literature

As we have seen in an earlier chapter, Robin Hood began his literary life in ballads of the late Middle Ages. At roughly the same time, he became established as a character in the May Games which took place throughout the country to welcome the arrival of summer. Both forms, the ballad and the mumming play, were ephemeral. The Robin Hood folk plays were local rituals, rarely written down and even more rarely preserved for later generations to read. The ballads may have been printed but they were not intended to survive for posterity. They were entertainments of and for the moment. Their writers would be astonished if they could know that some of their productions are still being read and studied four and five centuries after they first appeared in print. It was only in the latter half of the sixteenth century that Robin Hood began to figure in more conventional literature. Writers who were familiar with the stories from the ballads and the games started to include Robin in their own works.

It is a pity that the greatest of English playwrights never chose to write about the greatest of English outlaws. Shakespeare clearly knew the tales and the characters who populated them. There is a throwaway reference to 'the bare scalp of Robin Hood's fat friar' in *Two Gentlemen of Verona* and another in *Henry IV Part Two* when Justice Silence, boozily crooning to himself, sings of 'Robin Hood, Scarlet and John'. In *As You Like It*, in many ways a tale of the greenwood without its most familiar inhabitants, the duke is compared to the outlaw. 'They say he is already in the

Forest of Arden,' a character remarks in the very first scene, 'and a many merry men with him; and there they live like the old Robin Hood of England. They say many young gentlemen flock to him every day, and fleet the time carelessly, as they did in the golden world.' In Shakespeare's mind, Robin is clearly associated with a kind of forest Arcadia. However, Stratford's greatest son did not make use of the legend in any more extensive way.

In fact, only two of Shakespeare's contemporaries produced dramatic works that have survived in which Robin Hood is one of the principal characters. (There is evidence of other plays that are no longer extant. A 'pastorall plesant commedie' called *Robin Hood and Little John*, for example, is entered in the Stationers Register in 1594 but has been lost. There are also plays such as *George A Greene* by Robert Greene and *Look About You*, written by an anonymous author and printed in 1600, in which Robin appears in a subsidiary role.) The first was Anthony Munday, a prolific author of the Elizabethan and Jacobean eras, who is credited with the writing of two plays entitled *The Downfall of Robert, Earl of Huntington* and *The Death of Robert, Earl of Huntington*. In truth, these plays, like so many of the dramas of the period, may well have had more than one author. The diary of the theatrical entrepreneur Philip Henslowe records that he paid Munday £5 for a Robin Hood play in February 1598 but a later entry indicates that another playwright Henry Chettle was paid a further 10s for 'the mending of the first parte of Robart Hoode'. Presumably the two plays that we have were, in some sense, collaborative works, although there is no doubt that Munday produced much more of the text than Chettle and it is his name that is usually associated with them. Both works were printed in 1601. The first of them, *The Downfall of Robert, Earl of Huntington*, is notable for the fact that its hero, the man who becomes known as Robin Hood, is a dispossessed aristocrat. The idea of the outlaw as a wronged nobleman is very familiar in later works, from nineteenth-century novels to twentieth-century films, but here is its first appearance in a work of art. The earliest hints that Robin might have been something other than a yeoman appear decades before *The Downfall of Robert, Earl of Huntington* – in the work of the historian John Major and in the 1569 *Chronicle at Large* by Richard Grafton, a printer and scholar, who summarised what Major had said and then went on to report, 'In an olde and auncient Pamphlet I finde this written of the sayd Robert Hood. This man (sayth he) discended of a nobel parentage: or rather beyng of a base stocke and linage, was for his manhoode and chivalry advaunced to the noble dignitie of an Erle.' However, it was Munday who first introduced the notion into a work of the imagination and he was the first to provide his hero with the title of the 'Earl of Huntington'.

The Downfall is not a particularly good play and it is only remembered today because of its subject matter. It opens with a curious scene in which Munday pretends that what we are about to see is written not by him but by the earlier Tudor poet John Skelton who is also supposed to be playing the role of Friar Tuck. Once this conceit is established and the main action of the drama is underway, Munday wastes no time in despatching his hero into exile in Sherwood. When he gets him there, however, he seems unsure what to do with him. The new gentrified Robin can't be seen indulging in the activities of the old yeoman Robin of the ballads. He can't rob and kill and persecute churchmen and noblemen in quite the same way when he now comes, like them, from the upper stratum of society. In the ballads, there was a class antagonism between the outlaw and his victims. In Munday's plays he comes from the same social group as his enemies and the confrontation between them must be based on personal feelings rather than class tensions. The result is that the story of Robin as outlaw and the romance between him and Marian, identified by Munday as the daughter of Lord Fitzwalter, becomes entangled with plotting and conspiracy between the noblemen surrounding Prince John. *The Downfall* must have been a successful play at the time since there was sufficient demand for a sequel to be written but *The Death* provides even less scope for the outlaw hero. In fact, Munday kills him off early in the drama (giving him an improbably extended death scene) and turns his attention to the tribulations of the bereaved Marian.

The second playwright of the period to approach the legend was Ben Jonson. Author of satirical comedies such as *Volpone* and *The Alchemist*, Jonson is often considered the most gifted of Shakespeare's contemporaries. *The Sad Shepherd, or A Tale of Robin Hood* was his last play, unfinished at his death in 1637. We have been left with two acts and a few scenes from what would eventually have been a five-act drama. In *The Sad Shepherd* almost all sense of Robin as a genuine outlaw and robber has been banished. In its place is Robin Hood as gentle and genteel lord of the forest, planning to preside over feasting and festivities for his followers. He welcomes his 'friends and neighbours to the jolly bower' and 'to the greenwood walks'. He invites them to 'awake/The nimble hornpipe and the timburine/And mix our songs and dances in the wood'. He acts like the courtly host of upper-class revels. Here too is Robin as devoted lover who spends far more time kissing and embracing Marian than he does engaging in the less lawful pursuits of a traditional outlaw. The celebrations in the forest are interrupted, and the play's plot set in motion, by two events. One is the arrival of Eglamour, the Sad Shepherd of the title, who believes that his lover Earine has fallen into the Trent near the mill belonging to Much's father and has been drowned. The other is the interference of a witch who disguises herself as Marian in order to abuse Robin and harass him and his guests. It is difficult to know where Jonson planned to take his play (although it was completed and staged in the late eighteenth century by an actor/writer named Francis Waldron) but what we have demonstrates that he had problems with the material. Once Robin is so thoroughly gentrified and taken away from the illegal and violent activities that fuel the narratives of the ballads, there is not a lot for him to do. In *The Sad Shepherd*, the figure that provides the play with its subtitle is in danger of being shunted into the background. Even his responsibilities for slaying the deer to feed his guests are passed on to Marian.

It was not just dramatists of the Jacobean and Caroline eras who were drawn to the stories of Robin Hood. As we have seen, anonymous scribblers continued to produce ballads, often naïve in language and versification, throughout the period but more sophisticated poets also began to recognise Robin's significance and to include him in their work. Michael Drayton's *Polyolbion* was first published in 1612, although the poet had been working on it since the late 1590s. The book is a huge poem which attempts to describe successively all the counties of England and Wales. Drayton imagines assorted topographical features (rivers, valleys, hills) boasting in verse of the traditions and myths associated with them and, in the section of his work about Nottinghamshire, Sherwood Forest itself sings of the exploits of the famous outlaw who lived there. Drayton assumes universal knowledge of Robin Hood and writes that, 'In this our spacious isle, I think there is not one/But he hath heard some talk of him and Little John'. He knows how extensive and wide-ranging the stories are ('The merry pranks he played, would ask an age to tell/And the adventures strange that Robin Hood befell') and he knows that one of the fundamental differences between Robin and other outlaws was his generosity and charity. 'What often times he tooke,' he writes, 'he shar'd amongst the poor.'

Twenty years after *Polyolbion* was published and a few years before Jonson set about working on *The Sad Shepherd*, a man named Martin Parker produced what was probably the most substantial work on Robin in the ballad tradition since the *Gest* one hundred and thirty years earlier. Parker was a professional ballad writer living in London. Records suggest that he may also have been an inn-keeper. Where anonymity hides the identities of most of those who produced the broadsides of the seventeenth and eighteenth centuries, his name was attached to *A True Tale of Robin Hood*, a poem of nearly five hundred lines that was first published in the 1630s and reprinted more than fifty years later. His work is a kind of fusion of the stories from several ballads into one narrative and was clearly aimed at a slightly more upmarket audience than the cheap, single-sheet broadsides sold on the streets and at fairs. The poem also shows clear signs that Parker knew Munday's two plays and borrowed the idea of an aristocratic Robin from them. Parker's Robin, like Munday's, is the one-time Earl of Huntington. Exiled to the forest for debt, he takes to outlawry with enthusiasm. His hatred for religious figures ('His chiefest spight to the clergie was') does not seem initially unusual and Parker's highlighting of his hero's anti-clerical credentials is unsurprising in an era which had little time for Catholic clergy, past or present. What *is* rather eye-catching is his casual reference to Robin castrating monks and friars ('Their stones [testicles] he made them leese [lose]'), a habit that no other ballad records. As a means of preventing clerical lechery and the fathering of bastard children, which the author claims was Robin's intention, it seems a bit extreme. In fact, as the poem progresses, Parker places more and more emphasis primarily on the outlaw's opposition to 'th'crewell clergie' and twists himself into knots trying to portray him as no real threat to state or rightful king. He 'never practised any thing/Against the common wealth', he assures his readers. His eagerness to assert the truth of the tales he is reporting is matched only by his desire to stress how impossible it would be for such lawlessness to take place now. 'We that live in these latter dayes/Of civill government,' he comments, 'have a hundred wayes/Such outlaws to prevent'. It all seems a little odd until one remembers that Parker was writing in an age when disobedience to the powers that be was no laughing matter. Charles I was on the throne and the Civil War was only a decade away when he published his *True Tale of Robin Hood*. An outlaw was an ambivalent hero even for a popular ballad and Parker, clearly more royalist than roundhead in the making, produced a Robin Hood tale for his time.

Equally rooted in its era is a strange little play published thirty years later than Parker's work, after all the upheavals of the Civil War, Cromwell's rule and the restoration of the king in 1660. Only just over 150 lines long and entitled *Robin Hood and his Crew of Souldiers*, the play, according to the title page of the edition printed in 1661, was 'acted at Nottingham on the day of His Sacred Majesties Corronation'. It shows Robin's acknowledgement of past crimes and acceptance of a pardon as a counterpart to the submission of former rebels to the new authority of the restored Charles II.

For a century after the publication of *Robin Hood and his Crew of Souldiers*, the stage was one of the principal places where Robin could be found. Ballads continued to be published and already existing ballads were gathered together in anthologies and 'garlands'. However, new depictions of the outlaw hero in this period were most likely to emerge from the world of the London theatre. Robin became a regular character in the ballad operas that were popular at the time and was just as likely to burst into song as to let fly an arrow. (The vast majority of these eighteenth-century works for the stage were notable more for their music than any other qualities and they are considered in the later chapter entitled 'Musical Robin'.) It was only later in the century that an entirely new chapter in the literary history of Robin Hood was begun and, paradoxically, it was initiated by someone who was primarily interested in looking back at older versions of the story.

In the second half of the eighteenth century, a fashion for the folk poetry of the past developed. James Macpherson's *The Works of Ossian*, supposedly verse by an ancient Celtic bard, was the literary sensation of the 1760s. Thomas Percy, a churchman and future bishop, published his *Reliques of Ancient Poetry* in the same decade which included a handful of references to the Robin Hood ballads. Other collections followed. The time was ripe for a re-assessment of all the Robin Hood ballads. In 1795, an eccentric scholar named Joseph Ritson published a book with the impressive title of *Robin Hood: A Collection of All the Ancient Poems, Songs, and Ballads, Now Extant Relative to That Celebrated English Outlaw: To Which are Prefixed Historical Anecdotes of His Life.* It remains one of the most significant volumes ever published on the subject of the outlaw of Sherwood. Born in Stockton-on-Tees in 1752, Ritson moved to London as a young man and he earned his living as a conveyancer. His real interest, however, was in literature and he soon gained a reputation as a savage critic of those whose opinions on the subject he disliked. He was no respecter of reputation and even Dr. Johnson, then an old man, was on the receiving end of Ritson's attacks, lambasted for what the younger writer claimed were glaring errors in his edition of Shakespeare. In his own life as well as in his literary opinions, Ritson was a man unafraid of marching to the beat of a different drum. He was a vegetarian at a time when not eating meat was unusual and one of the last of his works published in his lifetime was entitled *An Essay on Abstinence from Animal Food, as a Moral Duty*; he was a political radical who welcomed the French Revolution and continued to express admiration for what the revolutionaries were doing long after other English supporters had lost their enthusiasm as a result of the excesses of the Terror. Quarrelsome and argumentative, Ritson was a man whose inability to get on with almost everybody often seemed close to pathological. In 1803, eight years after the publication of his great work on Robin, he did indeed lose his mind. After barricading himself in his lodgings and trying to burn all his manuscripts, he was removed to an asylum at Hoxton where, within a short time, he died.

It is difficult to overemphasise the importance of Ritson's work both in establishing the canon of Robin Hood literature from earlier centuries and in providing a sourcebook for those writers in later years who wanted to reinterpret and re-work that canon. Before Ritson there was a chaos of material which no scholar had properly organised; after him there was no comparable collection until the American Francis Child published his edition of the *Gest* and other ballads in 1888. The irascible scholar not only gathered together previously scattered material on the outlaw. He also provided his own interpretation of Robin Hood which has proved influential for more than two centuries. To Ritson, the reader of Tom Paine and the enthusiast for the French Revolution, Robin was a hero for all radicals. He was a man, as he wrote, 'who, in a barbarous age, and under a complicated tyranny, displayed a spirit of freedom and independence which has endeared him to the common people, whose cause he maintained (for all opposition to tyranny is the cause of the people), and, in spite of the malicious endeavours of pitiful monks, by whom history was consecrated to the crimes and follies of titled ruffians and sainted idiots, to suppress all record of his patriotic exertions and virtuous acts, will render his name immortal.'

In the decades following the publication of Ritson's massive work, and largely because of it, there was a resurgence of interest in Robin Hood. Writers of the Romantic era found much to attract them in the old legends and in the ballad form. In 1820, Leigh Hunt, perhaps best known today as a radical journalist and editor who was imprisoned for mocking the Prince Regent as a 'fat Adonis of forty', wrote four poems about Robin Hood in imitation of the medieval ballads he had read and admired. Reflecting

Hunt's own political beliefs, these show Robin as a champion of the poor and social justice, killing a deer in order to feed a starving peasant and defying corrupt churchmen, but they also celebrate the freedom and idealised community of the greenwood. 'How Robin and his Outlaws Lived in the Woods' describes, in cheery near-doggerel, the round of drinking, feasting, fighting and dancing in which Robin and his merry men engage. It was this liberating loosening of social constraints, as much as any political radicalism that could be read into the legend, that writers of the Romantic era found so appealing. Two years before Hunt published his poems in one of the magazines he edited, a minor poet named John Hamilton Reynolds wrote two sentimental sonnets in which he mourned the disappearance of 'the sweet days of merry Robin Hood'. He sent them to a friend for his opinion. The friend was John Keats. In a reply to Reynolds, Keats included his own verse on the subject of Robin Hood. Keats, of course, was a much superior poet to both Reynolds and Hunt and his lines have a sophistication and ambiguity that neither of them could match. He has sympathy with the longing for an imagined past that features so strongly in his friend's two poems but he turns his back on it. 'No! those days are gone away,' the very first line of Keats's poem proclaims and, although he may regret their departure and be more than prepared to give, 'Honour to bold Robin Hood/Sleeping in the underwood', he clearly sees little value in the kind of nostalgic musings in which Reynolds indulges.

Another Romantic, the later Poet Laureate Robert Southey, was drawn to the Robin Hood story throughout his life. As early as 1804, when he was casting around for a suitable subject for the English epic he was planning, he considered the possibility of using the outlaw leader but finally decided that Robin was not sufficiently elevated a topic for his purpose. He 'lowers the key too much', Southey wrote to a friend, although he continued to nurse the ambition to write a Robin Hood poem for decades to come. All that ever saw the light of day were a few fragments of a longer work and these were only published in a volume edited by his second wife that appeared in 1847, four years after his death.

Thomas Love Peacock's short novel *Maid Marian* was published in 1822 but, as its author was keen to point out in an authorial note, perhaps to avoid accusations of pinching ideas and characters from Sir Walter Scott's *Ivanhoe* (see below), much of it was written in 1818. The book is a curious combination of political satire and the same kind of romantic yearning for the simple pleasures of the greenwood that animates the poetry by Reynolds, Hunt and, in a more self-conscious way, Keats. For much of the first half of the book, Robin himself is an offstage presence and, even when he does put in an appearance in the second half to take his place in Peacock's cleverly concise versions of some of the most familiar stories from the ballads, he is a singularly colourless character. Peacock puts far more creative energy into Brother Michael, the obstreperous and eloquent man of the cloth who is later revealed to be the character we know as Friar Tuck, and into the depiction of his eponymous heroine. He is an ingenious writer but much of his wit is dependent on a knowledge of debates and ideas in Regency society which few now have and *Maid Marian* is not an easy read today. Arguably its most important and influential element is the love triangle it establishes between Robin Hood, Maid Marian and the chief villain, a plot device that has been played out in dozens and dozens of adaptations in the years since 1822.

Of all the Romantic writers who found inspiration in the legends, by far the most influential was Sir Walter Scott. Scott had known and admired Ritson. Indeed, he was one of the few literary friends with whom the easily offended scholar never fell out. Scott himself was fascinated by the ballad form and one of the most successful of his early works, *The Minstrelsy of the Scottish*

Border, was a collection of the songs and ballads of Lowland Scotland. When he turned his attention to fiction, it was probably inevitable that sooner or later he would draw upon the Robin Hood material that his late friend Ritson had gathered together twenty years earlier. The only surprise is that the outlaw does not play a more central role than he does in *Ivanhoe*, the sixth in Scott's series of 'Waverley' novels but the first to take its inspiration from English rather than Scottish history. Published in 1819, the book focuses not on Locksley, as Scott calls his Robin Hood figure, who appears in no more than ten of its forty-four chapters, but on the fortunes of the Saxon nobles Cedric of Rotherwood and his son Wilfred of Ivanhoe. Locksley supports the Saxons in their fight against the villainous Templar Brian de Bois-Guilbert but he is not a central character. And yet, despite this, it is undoubtedly true to say that *Ivanhoe*, apart possibly from Howard Pyle's 1883 book *The Merry Adventures of Robin Hood*, is the single most important Robin Hood text of the nineteenth century.

In two significant respects, Scott's presentation of Locksley/Robin Hood in the novel has shaped the way the outlaw hero has been seen ever since. In casting Robin Hood as a champion of the Saxons against the Normans and in setting the outlaw's story firmly in the reign of Richard the Lionheart, he established a template which has been used time and again by other writers and, more recently, by filmmakers. Not only that but also, over the years, Robin has taken on some of the attributes of the eponymous hero of Scott's novel. Like Wilfred of Ivanhoe, but unlike the outlaw of the ballads, Robin Hood is often portrayed in books and films as a warrior returning from the Crusades. Even in the smaller incidents of *Ivanhoe*, Scott created motifs that have become a familiar part of later re-tellings of the story. One of the novel's great set-pieces is the tournament at Ashby-de-la-Zouch where the knights display their prowess and an archery contest is part of the entertainment. One competitor hits the centre of the target and seems unbeatable but he is topped by Locksley who splits the arrow in the bullseye. How often has that miraculous feat of toxophily been acted and re-enacted over the years? Whether one looks at the larger sweep of the narrative or at the smaller details of the plot, *Ivanhoe* reveals itself as a crucial work in the development of the Robin Hood story. In the 1810s and 1820s, Scott was creating the tradition of the historical novel almost single-handedly and it was of great importance to Robin that the outlaw should have been made a part of that tradition. Thanks to Scott's decision to place him in the story of *Ivanhoe*, he became much more readily available as a character for other nineteenth-century writers of historical fiction to employ.

None of these was a match for Scott in literary quality but some of them produced work that reached a large audience. *Robin Hood and Little John or, The Merry Men of Sherwood Forest* by Pierce Egan the Younger was published in weekly serialisation in 1839 and 1840 and in a single, huge volume in the latter year. Pierce Egan the Elder was one of the best-known authors of the Regency Era, a pioneering sportswriter with a particular interest in the prize fights of the day and the creator of the original 'Tom and Jerry', two men about town in his 1821 work *Life in London*. His son, also named Pierce Egan, was never as famous as his father but he became a prolific journalist and novelist in the Victorian era. His Robin Hood novel, published soon after another excursion into the medieval era entitled *Wat Tyler*, was one of his most successful and remains a lively read even today. Unlike Scott, Egan opts for a noble Robin, making the outlaw hero (as he is so often) the son of the Earl of Huntingdon and involving him in a series of breathlessly told adventures in the greenwood. *Robin Hood and Little John* was reprinted several times in the middle decades of the nineteenth century. Its popularity even survived a journey across the Channel. Two books usually attributed to Alexandre Dumas, *Le Prince des Voleurs* (*The Prince of Thieves*) and *Robin*

Hood le Proscrit (Robin Hood the Outlaw), both published in France in the 1870s, are actually little more than translated adaptations of Egan's work with Dumas's name attached to them. The likelihood is that Dumas knew the original book and suggested to the publisher that a French edition might sell, perhaps also suggesting a translator. He then agreed to lend his name to the project to provide it with more publicity.

Other similar novels followed Egan's. Joachim H. Stocqueler's *Maid Marian, the Forest Queen* was published in 1849 and focused, as its title makes clear, on Robin's adventurous inamorata who has become 'queen of the wood' while her lover is away in the Holy Land. Stocqueler was a prolific journalist and intrepid traveller, many of whose other books recorded his adventures in Central Asia, Afghanistan and India. His great contribution to the Robin Hood story is that, combining the characteristics of two figures from *Ivanhoe* (Locksley and Ivanhoe himself), he established the outlaw as a returned crusader. *Maid Marian, the Forest Queen* is almost certainly the first novel in which Robin has fought against the Saracens in the Middle East and the idea soon became a common one. It has persisted to the present day. In the recent BBC TV series, for example, the hero is, to a great extent, defined by his experiences in the Holy Land.

One of the appeals of Robin in the Victorian era was his flexibility. He could be the hero of melodramatic fiction like Egan's or Stocqueler's. He could also mean something to both conservative and radical poets. To a romantic revolutionary like the wood engraver, poet and republican activist WJ Linton, the character could seem like a reminder of more human values on which the age had turned its back. In a lyric dating from 1865, Linton yearned 'for the life of Robin Hood, to wander an outlaw free/Rather than crawl in the market-place of human slavery'. Robin becomes a symbol of what has been lost in the Industrial Revolution, someone who lived 'out of the noisome smoke' and 'where the earth breathes fragrantly'. To Alfred, Lord Tennyson, Poet Laureate and (in most ways) pillar of the establishment, he was a representative of traditional English virtues. Tennyson turned his attention to Robin in a drama entitled *The Foresters*. He first wrote it, in a mixture of verse and prose, in the early 1880s. His previous play had been staged by Henry Irving at the Lyceum Theatre and he expected that this one would also be performed there. However, Irving thought it insufficiently dramatic and rejected it. Tennyson put the play on one side. Only in 1892, the last year of his life, was *The Foresters* staged and then it was in New York. American audiences liked it and productions in other American cities followed. Unfortunately, when it was performed in London a year later, after Tennyson's death, English theatregoers were less impressed and tended to agree with Irving's assessment of it a decade earlier. *The Foresters* lasted only seventeen performances.

In the century and more since its premiere, most writers on Tennyson's work have dismissed it, one critic in the 1950s even wearily asking the question, 'How did the author of *The Idylls of the King* come to put his name to such puerile rubbish?' Read today, *The Foresters* is more interesting than such savage condemnation suggests. It undoubtedly has major faults. The plot, once Robin and Marian have fled to the greenwood, rapidly runs out of steam and it is not difficult to see why Irving considered the piece undramatic. There is far too much heavy-handed 'humour' of the kind which, for example, sees Robin, disguised as an old hag, swapping dull banter with the sheriff and Prince John. There are some irritating scenes in which Little John woos Marian's maidservant. When Robin falls asleep, dreaming of the arrival on stage of the fairy queen Titania and her followers, the audience is treated to some of Tennyson's least effective verse ever ('We be fairies of the wood/We be neither bad nor good'). And yet *The Foresters* neatly embodies some of the nineteenth century's most typical attitudes to the outlaw leader. Here is Robin as the vehicle for a very straightforward Victorian patriotism. When the foresters, at the beginning of Act 2, sing that, 'There is no land like England,/Where'er the light of day be;/There are no hearts like English hearts,/Such hearts of oak as they be', they are not inviting the audience's ironic scepticism. They are anticipating its complete agreement with the sentiments they express. Here is the gentrified Robin, firmly established as the Earl of Huntington, who is unjustly exiled to the forest by the bad guys. (Although the outlaw hero turns his back on his aristocratic status once he takes to the woods. 'Nay, no earl am I,' he says, 'I am English yeoman.' In the final analysis, whether noble or not, it is Robin's essential Englishness that is important.) Here is Robin the chaste lover of Maid Marian. Here is Robin as the embodiment of the natural world who soliloquises about the wonders of the 'free forest life' in contrast to the chafing restrictions of existence 'among my thralls in baronial hall'. So many of the ideas about the outlaw that were either established or developed in the course of the nineteenth century find expression in Tennyson's drama. In his telling of the Robin Hood story, the poet proves himself, as elsewhere in his work, eminently Victorian.

Tennyson's engagement with the Robin Hood stories shows that he could be seen by Victorians as a serious subject for adult literature. And yet it was the nineteenth century that also saw the transformation of Robin into a figure from children's literature. How did he come to be seen as primarily a character for the young to read about? In the early decades of the nineteenth century there were certainly versions of the stories that were very obviously aimed at a juvenile readership. Alfred Mills's 1825 volume *Sherwood Forest*, for example, begins with the author's address to 'my little friends' and re-tells some of the familiar ballad tales (the meeting between Robin and Little John, Robin's adventure with the tinker) in straightforward, simple prose.

Looking at the book today, it is striking how robust children's imaginations were assumed to be in the 1820s. Mills's book is illustrated by a number of crudely coloured wood engravings, one showing Robin lopping off an opponent's head which tumbles to the ground. It's a good deal more graphic than anything that might have been used twenty years later as the illustration for a children's book.

As the century went on, the market for children's literature gradually developed and it was the Victorian era that increasingly saw the publication of titles on Robin Hood intended solely for the young. The first of these was Stephen Percy's *Robin Hood and His Merry Foresters,* published in 1841. 'Stephen Percy' was the pen-name of Joseph Cundall, a significant figure in the history of children's literature, both as author and publisher, and a pioneering photographer who was one of the founders in 1853 of the Royal Photographic Society. Cundall begins his book with the simple statement that, 'Tales of Robin Hood and his merry foresters were the delight of my boyhood' and his aim is clearly to pass on that delight to a new generation. Passing off the stories in the volume as transcriptions of the tales he told his schoolfellows many years before, he produces a lively version of the Robin Hood of the ballads and broadsides, mixed with his own, occasional inventions.

Robin Hood and His Merry Foresters was reprinted several times in the course of the nineteenth century and other novels for boys followed but, as the expert on Robin Hood in children's literature Kevin Carpenter points out, 'the number of books presenting his life and adventures for young readers in the nineteenth century is surprisingly low.' There is a seeming paradox here. Robin was becoming a hero fit only for children and yet many children's publishers and writers were wary of him. Given the long-lasting popularity of the outlaw hero, the exceptional growth in the market for children's books during

Victoria's reign and the desire to find patriotic heroes for young people to admire, this is indeed strange. The possibility is that Robin made some Victorian children's writers uncomfortable. Here was an English hero, undoubtedly, but a hero who was also an outlaw and a robber. Was he really a role model for the young?

The solution to the apparent paradox – that Robin became a central figure in many children's reading lives at the same time that many publishers and writers shied away from him – lies in the kind of literature in which he featured. For much of the century, Robin was as likely to be found between the covers of penny dreadfuls, jostling for space with the likes of Sweeney Todd, Dick Turpin and Varney the Vampire, as he was in the pages of books hot off the presses of more respectable publishers. The 1860s saw the development of commercially successful boys' weeklies, retailing at a penny, and an increased production of fiction, published in weekly instalments, also at a penny. The first penny-part Robin Hood novel aimed specifically at boys was George Emmett's *Robin Hood and the Outlaws of Sherwood Forest* which was published in 52 weekly instalments during 1868 and 1869. Emmett's re-telling of the story, which he claims comes from intensive research in old manuscripts and archives but actually owes most to a reading of Ritson, is lively and melodramatic. The language is full of fine-sounding archaisms ('A malison on thee, thou knave of the blackest dye'), the narrative is full of fighting, feasting and boozing, and Robin himself is a vigorous hero, as eager to perform astonishing feats of archery as he is to battle against Norman tyranny. Curiously, Emmett sets his story in the 1260s, after Simon de Montfort's defeat at the Battle of Evesham, a time when rivalry between Saxon and Norman was even more of an anachronism than it was in those novels, like *Ivanhoe*, set in the reign of Richard I.

Over the next thirty years, Robin and His Merry Men entertained young readers in stories, usually in serial form, published in a succession of boys' weeklies with titles like *Boys of England*, *Young Britannia*, *The Young Briton* and *Young Men of Great Britain*. As the names suggest, these might have been dismissed by harsher critics as penny dreadfuls but they were also patriotic productions, designed to inculcate a sturdy love of country in their juvenile readers. The details of these serial stories may be different – and they lent themselves to all kinds of variations and alternative versions – but the fundamental plotlines remain the same. Damsels in distress, usually but not always called Marian, are rescued; the dastardly deeds of the Normans bring down the vengeance of Robin and his men; the rich and proud are robbed and brought low; the poor and deserving are the recipients of the Merry Men's charity. Interestingly, in a foretaste of what *Robin of Sherwood* was to offer a century later, many of these stories also include elements of the supernatural – woodland demons and spirits of Sherwood who provide the hero with the kind of magical assistance that Herne the Hunter does in the TV series.

By the end of the Victorian era, the penny dreadful had run its course. New boys' magazines had emerged to replace it, most of them published by Alfred Harmsworth, later Lord Northcliffe. In AA Milne's memorable words, Harmsworth 'killed the penny dreadful by the simple process of producing the ha'penny dreadfuller'. Dreadfuller these cheaper titles may have been but they proved less welcoming to Robin. Only a handful of outlaw stories appeared in Harmsworth titles in the Edwardian period and, although his Amalgamated Press published a *Robin Hood Library* immediately after the First World War, by then the fashion in boy's weekly fiction was for school stories and tales of modern adventure rather than historical romance. In fact, during the Edwardian era and the interwar years Robin largely migrated from cheap magazines into the pages of more prestigious, hardcover books, often lavishly and skilfully illustrated. Victorian concerns about the suitability of the outlaw as a hero for the young began to disappear.

The trend had first shown itself in the last decades of the nineteenth century and the most influential of all these more upmarket versions of the stories was actually by an American. Howard Pyle was an illustrator and author, born in Delaware in 1853. *The Merry Adventures of Robin Hood*, published in 1883, was his first great success and it has continued to attract readers for more than 125 years. It has never been out of print and it has appeared in literally hundreds of editions. Part of its appeal lies in the illustrations. Pyle was a skilled draughtsman with an ability to combine romance and realism, which was ideally suited to the depiction of adventure stories like the Robin Hood tales. One unexpected enthusiast for Pyle's work was Vincent van Gogh who wrote in a letter to his brother Theo that he had seen some of the American's illustrations in *Harper's Magazine* and had been struck 'dumb with admiration'. However, it is Pyle's breezy text that really distinguishes *The Merry Adventures of Robin Hood* from earlier books like those by Stephen Percy and George Emmett. His book still has an energy and vitality that nearly all its predecessors lack. He takes much of his material from what he calls the 'goodly ballads of the olden time' but he smooths down any rough edges and creates a late romantic idyll of life in the greenwood. In Pyle's version, Robin and his men are like overgrown boys, breaking off from their feasting and fun in Sherwood only to play violent pranks on one another or on the Sheriff and his men. Women have scarcely any role to play at all. Maid Marian is mentioned only twice and is conspicuous only by her absence from the stories. Pyle's book is also a relentlessly cheery re-telling of the tales (seldom has any text made such frequent use of the word 'merry' in a few hundred pages) and it is written in the kind of *faux* medieval language that was common enough in historical fiction of the period. Thees, thous and thys are scattered throughout the chapters, people rarely simply 'say' anything but 'quoth' regularly and 'God wot' is the interjection of choice. None of this gets in the way of Pyle's ability to tell a story. His tales of Robin are, quite simply, enormous fun and it is not difficult, reading them today, to understand why they have proved so successful. His bestseller was not, of course, the first book about Robin Hood published in the USA but it played a hugely significant role in the adoption by Americans of the English outlaw as, in some way, a cultural hero of their own. It is impossible to imagine Robin Hood in the twentieth century without the versions of his story produced in America and it is almost equally impossible to imagine that most of them would have come into existence had it not been for the popularity of *The Merry Adventures of Robin Hood*. Without Howard Pyle's book, there would probably have been no Hollywood films about Robin.

Other artists and writers in the USA followed in Pyle's pioneering tracks. J. Walker McSpadden's *Stories of Robin Hood and His Merry Outlaws*, published in 1904, also made extensive use of the old ballads and indeed prefaced each chapter with a quote, in updated English, from one of them. Louis Rhead was an English-born illustrator who settled in New York in his twenties and went on to become a naturalised US citizen. His *Bold Robin Hood and his Outlaw Band* was published in 1912. Paul Creswick's *Robin Hood*, which appeared five years later, had illustrations by NC Wyeth, perhaps the best-known graduate of the art school Pyle had established in his home town of Wilmington, Delaware and the father of Andrew Wyeth, one of twentieth-century America's most admired painters. Charlotte Harding, who provided the illustrations for *Robin Hood: His Book* by the then well-known children's writer Eva March Tappan in 1903, was another artist who had studied with Pyle in Wilmington.

Meanwhile, back in Britain, the last flickers of nineteenth-century romanticism's interest in Robin Hood could still be glimpsed in the work of some Edwardian writers. John Drinkwater wrote a short play entitled *Robin Hood and the Pedlar* and Alfred Noyes produced a number of poems on the subject of the outlaw. Noyes's fame has not lasted, although many will know his narrative poem of 1906 entitled 'The Highwayman', but the best of his Robin Hood poems, called simply 'Sherwood', is a spirited exercise in nostalgia in which the poet imagines the heroes of the greenwood returning to life in the contemporary forest. He also wrote a play about Robin, first published in 1911, entitled *Sherwood or Robin Hood and the Three Kings*. This is an odd exercise in pseudo-Shakespearean, or perhaps more accurately pseudo-Tennysonian, blank verse in which the outlaw leader and his merry men share the stage with Oberon and Titania, the fairy king and queen familiar from *A Midsummer Night's Dream*. Robin is once again identified as the Earl of Huntingdon. The Sheriff of Nottingham becomes a minor character and the chief villains in Noyes's drama are Prince John and his mother Queen Elinor. The prince lusts after Maid Marian while the queen schemes and plots against Robin. In the final act, both Robin and Marian die at Kirklees Priory, victims of their royal enemies, but they are last seen, triumphing over death, as they join Titania and Oberon in their immortal fairyland. The play now seems a strange marriage of very different legends of the greenwood but it was staged several times in the years just before and just after the First World War. It must have struck some sort of chord with his contemporaries.

Although it may not be always apparent reading them today, Drinkwater and Noyes were aiming their works at adults but nearly all the other authors of the period who produced Robin Hood tales wrote them for children. In most people's minds, Robin was firmly established by the early twentieth century as a subject fit only for juvenile literature. Books with titles like *Robin Hood and His Merry Outlaws* and *Tales of the Greenwood* began to proliferate and most of the major publishers for children had at least one Robin Hood book on their lists. Some of these Edwardian-era volumes have had surprisingly long lives. Henry Gilbert's *Robin Hood and the Men of the Greenwood*, originally published in 1912, was still in bookshops as a 'Wordsworth Children's Classic' in the 1990s. New children's books about Robin continued to appear regularly in the interwar years. Charles Henry Cannell, a prolific English author of all kinds of genre fiction from detective stories to 'lost world' novels, published a re-telling of the tales in 1927 under one of his many pen-names, E. Charles Vivian. Carola Oman, daughter of the military historian Sir Charles Oman, wrote a volume on the outlaw for JM Dent's Children's Classics series in 1937 which was still being reprinted decades later. A far better writer than either Cannell or Oman also took an idiosyncratic interest in the legends. With a blithe disregard for even a semblance of historical accuracy TH White included Robin Hood in his Arthurian novel *The Sword in the Stone*, first published in 1938. Under the name of Robin Wood, the outlaw is one of those figures encountered by the young Arthur during his education by the wizard Merlin.

Perhaps the most interesting of all these inter-war versions of the stories is *Bows Against the Barons* by Geoffrey Trease, first published in 1934. Like many young writers in the 1930s, Trease was on the left and his radical sympathies are very clear in what was his first novel. The narrative follows Dickon, a teenage boy who kills one of the king's deer and flees into Sherwood Forest. There he joins Robin Hood and is present as the outlaw leader organises a large-scale peasants' revolt against the oppression of the local lord Sir Rolf D'Eyncourt and others of his ilk. At times the book reads almost like left-wing propaganda. When he lectures his merry men on the virtues of equality ('All men are equal in the forest... They should be equal in the whole world. They should work for themselves and for each other – not for some master set over them.') Robin Hood sounds less like a hero of the greenwood and more like an eloquent member of the Nottingham Communist Party in full flow. It is no great surprise to learn that the book was immensely popular in the Soviet Union and that Trease was able to spend five months travelling there in 1935 on the strength of his Russian royalties. What rescues *Bows Against the Barons* from tedious didacticism is the narrative skill and vivid writing which Trease went on to demonstrate in more than a hundred other historical novels over the course of a literary career that lasted into the 1990s. Whatever one thinks about his first book, it's all very different from Enid Blyton who, perhaps surprisingly, also produced a version of the Robin Hood stories in the 1930s.

After the Second World War, Robin's continuing popularity, combined with the release of the Disney film and the screening of the Richard Greene series, meant that there was no shortage of new children's books about the outlaw. Some were directly based on the movie or the TV series and were often illustrated by stills. Others were more substantial and imaginative works. One of the very earliest books written by the historian Antonia Fraser, now known for biographies of Cromwell and Mary, Queen of Scots and for her memoir of her marriage to Harold Pinter, was a re-telling of the Robin Hood stories. Published under her maiden name of Antonia Pakenham in 1955, this appeared in a new edition in 1971 with illustrations by her then teenage daughter Rebecca, now a biographer and historian herself. Rosemary Sutcliff is most famous as the author of *The Eagle of the Ninth*, a story set in Roman Britain that was recently made into a film, but her first published book, appearing in 1950, was *The Chronicles of Robin Hood*. Commissioned by Oxford University Press after an editor there had seen a manuscript of Celtic legends Sutcliff had submitted to the publisher, this is a fine version of the traditional stories, much enhanced by the illustrations of C. Walter Hodges. The most influential of 1950s books about Robin, largely because it was in print so long as a Puffin and a Puffin Classic, was Roger Lancelyn Green's *The Adventures of Robin Hood*. For several generations of British children, this was the book that was most likely to provide them with their introduction to the stories. It is a conventional but skilful re-working of the old ballads into narratives suitable for children. Lancelyn Green was a friend of CS Lewis, whose biography he wrote, and a member of the Oxford literary group the Inklings, which also included JRR Tolkien amongst its members. As a writer he came to specialise in the re-telling of myths and legends for younger readers and his bibliography also includes titles on Arthurian stories, Greek myths, Ancient Egyptian mythology and stories of the Norse Gods. His Robin is rooted in a real medieval world but Green also emphasises the hero's mythic status as a champion of the poor and exemplar of justice and fairness.

Throughout the second half of the last century, Robin continued to thrive in children's books. Film and TV versions of the story, such as Disney's feature-length cartoon of 1973 and the *Robin of Sherwood* series in the 1980s, provided the pegs on which publishers could hang new volumes but they really needed no excuse. Robin, still one of the most immediately recognisable figures from English folklore or history, could be relied upon to return any investment made in books about him. Story books, picture books, easy reading books with simplified vocabulary, audiobooks, Robin Hood annuals, books in which characters from the Muppets took the parts of the heroes of Sherwood, role-playing game-books – all appeared at some time in the seventies and eighties. Even during the last twenty years, when the children's market has become so competitive and so dominated by fantasy, Robin has certainly not vanished. And some of the most admired writers for children in recent decades have produced their own versions of his story. Michael Morpurgo, Children's Laureate between 2003 and 2005, published *Robin of*

Sherwood in 1996. This is a clever re-working of the legend which begins in the present when a young blind boy discovers a medieval skull that has been brought to the surface of the earth in the aftermath of a storm. As he handles it, the boy is thrown back into a vision of the past in which he has become Robin, an outcast fighting for survival in the forest. Monica Furlong's *Robin's Country* from 1994 tells the story from the point of view of a mute orphan boy who stumbles on the outlaws' camp after he is driven into Sherwood by the cruelty of his master.

For much of the last century, then, Robin was seen as a character suited only to juvenile literature. The total number of Robin Hood titles aimed at children ran into the hundreds. The number intended to be read primarily by adults was negligible. One of the very few was *The Good Yeomen* by the American historian and novelist Jay Williams which was first published in 1948. Told from the point of view of Little John, a blacksmith who kills a man and flees into the forest where he encounters Robin, this is a book which neatly intertwines reworked material from the ballads, particularly the *Gest*, and the author's own inventions, most notably a female character named Lady Agnes with whom both Robin and John fall in love. However, in recent decades, the unwritten rule that Robin Hood is suitable only for younger readers has changed. Since about 1980, all kinds of new versions of the outlaw leader have begun to appear in fiction written for adult readers. Robin has been reinvented in a succession of different guises. Most of these novels of the last three decades have fallen, unsurprisingly, into the broad category of historical fiction, although there have been Robin stories that fit more readily into other genres. And there have been two very noticeable trends in Robin Hood fiction. Firstly, some writers, nearly all women, have found imaginative means to reinterpret the legends from a feminist standpoint. This has usually, although not always, involved the transformation and adaptation of the character of

Maid Marian. Secondly, there have been writers, nearly all men, who have overturned the idea of the outlaw as chivalric hero and presented Robin in their fiction as an amoral, even thuggish figure.

Nicholas Chase's *Locksley*, published in 1983, was one of the first books to reclaim Robin Hood as a character for adult historical fiction. Taking a format that has often been used in historical novels (the central character, as an old man or woman, sits down to write his memoirs), the author produced a clever narrative that intertwines the legend with the real history of the late twelfth and early thirteenth centuries. Nicholas Chase, actually a pseudonym for two brothers, Christopher and Anthony Hyde, chose the most common period in which to set the story and its hero, despite the new adventures in which he was involved, was recognisably the familiar Robin of myth and legend. Other writers have made more radical changes to the basic material. Parke Godwin's 1991 novel *Sherwood* overturns tradition by setting the story not in the era of Good King Richard and Bad King John but in the years immediately following the Norman Conquest. Robin in this version is Edward of Denby, a Saxon thane forced from his land in the wake of William the Conqueror's invasion, who takes refuge in Sherwood Forest and becomes known as 'Robin Hood'. Godwin, who had previously written a trilogy of novels re-interpreting the Arthurian legends in the context of the Roman departure from Britain, had a certain historical logic on his side in that the bitter confrontation between Saxon and Norman, so long a central part of the Robin Hood story, makes more sense in the immediate aftermath of the Conquest than it does in the late twelfth century. *Sherwood* was followed two years later by a sequel entitled *Robin and the King*.

Like Parke Godwin, Stephen Lawhead sets his 'King Raven' trilogy (*Hood*, *Scarlet*, *Tuck*) in the years immediately after the Norman Conquest but he transfers the stories to the border region between Wales and England. Lawhead's previous work included the 'Pendragon Cycle', a sequence of novels re-telling the Arthurian legends in a firmly Celtic context, but the attempt to do something similar for Robin Hood (his Hood figure is a Welsh princeling named Bran ap Brychan) can sometimes seem wilfully perverse. Robin is fundamentally an English figure in a way that Arthur need not necessarily be and it is very difficult to recast him as Celtic. Michael Cadnum's *In a Dark Wood*, published in 1998, looks at the legend through the eyes of the Sheriff of Nottingham. Marketed as a 'young adult' novel, this is a narrative that succeeds rather well in turning the traditional story on its head and allowing readers to sympathise with the Sheriff and his teenage squire rather than any of the outlaws they must face. *Forbidden Forest*, published four years later, is by the same author and returns to the legend. Once again Cadnum uses not Robin but another character (this time Little John) as the focus for his story.

With the noticeable increase in popularity of historical crime fiction over the past three decades, it was inevitable that so familiar a character as Robin Hood would be hijacked for use in mystery novels. *The Assassin in the Greenwood* by PC Doherty has the author's recurring character Hugh Corbett investigating the murders of royal tax collectors and a sheriff in Nottingham. Corbett is soon on the track of Robin of Locksley, an outlaw previously pardoned by the king who has returned to his old haunts in Sherwood Forest. Interestingly, Doherty, a medieval historian by training, chooses to set his Robin Hood story in the reign of Edward I rather than the time of Richard the Lionheart and adds an afterword to it in which he argues vigorously that this is the correct chronology for the outlaw. Clayton Emery is an American author who has been drawn repeatedly to the outlaw legend over the course of his writing career. Since the late 1980s he has published new 'Tales of Robin Hood', many of which involve the outlaw hero in *Robin of Sherwood*-style encounters with magic and sorcery, but his most original contributions to the modern development of the character are probably the stories published in magazines in the States in which Robin and Marian act as detectives. In a typical example like 'Dowsing the Demon', which first appeared in 'Ellery Queen's Mystery Magazine' in November 1994, Robin and Marian are visiting Lincoln to buy cloth to make new outfits for the Merry Men when they are drawn into the furore surrounding a double murder in the town.

Even science fiction, fantasy and horror, unlikely genres to accommodate a medieval outlaw, have their examples of Robin Hood fiction. Esther Friesner's *The Sherwood Game*, for instance, is a novel in which Robin is a character in a computer game created by a nerdish programmer named Carl Sherwood. During the course of Friesner's largely predictable but occasionally entertaining narrative, Robin escapes from the game and joins Carl in the real world. As noted above, some of Clayton Emery's Robin Hood stories contain elements of fantasy and Emery was also one of the contributors to a 1991 American anthology entitled *The Fantastic Adventures of Robin Hood* which despatched Robin into space and plunged him into other SF and horror narratives. The recent *Robin Hood vs the Plague Undead* is a book for older children which cheerfully mashes up different genres into an oddly satisfying brew and tells the story of what happens when Robin has to battle against the zombies that Prince John has recruited to fight for his claim to the throne.

Feminist versions of Robin have provided some of the most interesting and original takes on the character in recent decades. Of course, Robin Hood fiction has not been an exclusively male preserve since at least the turn of the twentieth century. *The Boy Foresters* by the appropriately named Anne Bowman, a novel which focuses on the adventures of three orphaned children who are taken in by Robin's outlaw band, was published in 1905 and, as we have seen, many of the children's versions of the stories that appeared between the 1920s and the 1950s were written by women. In the last thirty years, female writers of all kinds have continued to find inspiration in Robin Hood in books aimed at children. Catherine Storr, author of the classic *Marianne Dreams*, provided the text for a picture book on Robin in 1984. *Rowan Hood*, by the prolific American author Nancy Springer, is the first of a series of books published in the last decade which feature a young girl, the unacknowledged daughter of the outlaw, who takes to Sherwood with her own gang to rival that of her father.

For some women writers of breathless historical romance, life in Sherwood has also had its attractions. Introduce a beautiful young woman into the midst of all those merry men and heaving bosoms and panting passion are soon in evidence. In Diane Carey's *Under the Wild Moon*, for example, the heroine arrives in the greenwood to join Robin's band. Little time passes before she is getting intimately acquainted with Will Scarlet ('she moaned with pleasure as his gentle touch made her forget that he was one of Robin Hood's bandits') and re-introducing him to delights that have long been absent from his outlaw life. Other novels, such as Gayle Feyrer's *The Thief's Mistress*, made the most of the opportunities offered by a love triangle between Marian, Robin and Sir Guy of Gisbourne.

However, it was those novels which tried to reinvent the legend from a feminist perspective that provided it with a genuinely new direction in which to travel. Robin McKinley's *The Outlaws of Sherwood* was published in 1988. In some ways, this seems like a fairly straightforward re-telling of the stories and it includes familiar elements (helping a knight named Sir Richard of the Lea to repay an unfairly arranged loan, combating a ruthless mercenary named Guy of Gisbourne) which go back as far as the old ballads. Most editions of the book carry a jacket illustration of Robin in traditional greenwood pose, dressed in Lincoln green and carrying his bow. And yet the characterisation of the outlaw is far from traditional. This is Robin as New Man, emotional and aware of the needs of others. No longer the brilliant archer of a thousand versions of the story, this Robin is a poor shot with the bow (he was outlawed in the first place because he accidentally killed a man with it when he merely intended to wound him) who realises that he stands no chance of winning the golden arrow in the Sheriff's archery contest. McKinley's Robin is an ordinary man transformed into hero almost by accident. The most forceful and memorable character in her book is undoubtedly Marian. A better archer than Robin, she bears no resemblance at all to the anaemic Marian, who appears in so many twentieth-century tellings of the tales, loitering in the background of the action and awaiting a word or smile from her paragon of a lover.

Jennifer Roberson's *Lady of the Forest*, which appeared five years after *The Outlaws of Sherwood*, has sometimes been packaged by its publishers to look very much like the kind of novel in which the Nottinghamshire earth will regularly move – on one dust jacket a hunk with flowing blond hair and shirt open to the waist is clutching a medieval maiden in an amorous embrace – but it is actually a more intriguing book than the cover designers suggest.

It is an attempt to do for the Robin Hood story what Marion Zimmer Bradley's *The Mists of Avalon* had done for the Arthurian legends – to give it a new relevance for a modern female readership – and, in most editions, it carries a recommendation from Bradley herself. Again Marian is the strongest character in the novel. Robin, in Roberson's book, has returned from the Crusades a damaged and haunted man and it is Marian who has the resources to support him as he struggles to turn himself into the hero we all know. Roberson returned to the legend half-a-dozen years later with *Lady of Sherwood*, set in the period just after the death of Richard the Lionheart when Prince John's accession to the throne changes the fortunes of the outlaw leader and his lover.

McKinley and Roberson are by no means the only women writers of the last few decades to turn their attention to the intertwined stories of Robin and Marian. In Elsa Watson's *Maid Marian* (2004), the heroine is a teenage widow, her fate in the hands of the king's mother Eleanor of Aquitaine, who flees to the forest to escape an arranged marriage and there begins to fall for the greenwood hero. Once again, the story revisits many of the familiar elements of the legend but they are all seen through the eyes of Marian who is very definitely the focus of the novel. Theresa Tomlinson published *The Forestwife* in 1993. Marketed to a young adult readership, it was, in many ways, the most radical of all the feminist reinterpretations of the Robin and Marian story. In Tomlinson's book, Marian is Mary de Holt, a fifteen-year-old girl who finds her destiny in Barnsdale when she inherits the role of forestwife, or herbalist and healer, from the old woman who takes her in. Adopting the name of Marian, she becomes the centre of a female community in counterpoint to Robin's band of men. She becomes the Green Lady of the Woods in the same way as Robin has so often been seen as the Green Man. She and Robin are close but there is no question of her relinquishing the position of forestwife to become no more than an outlaw's submissive helpmeet. This is Marian as career woman whose life has a significance and a purpose that are not dependent on her relationship to Robin. Tomlinson has gone on to publish two more volumes – *Child of the May* and *The Path of the She Wolf* – which further follow the characters from *The Forestwife*.

As women writers have explored ideas of a feminist Maid Marian and reinvented Robin as a 'New Man', what have male writers been making of the story in recent years? One response has been to emphasise the brutality of the era in which it is set. In some ways, this is a return to the Robin of the ballads. As we saw in an earlier chapter, the world revealed in a work like 'Robin Hood and the Monk', with its casual violence and murder, is far from the familiar image of greenwood chivalry we all recognise. Yet there is also a new insistence in recent fiction that Sherwood must have been a place where life was all too likely to be nasty, brutish and short and that, to survive and thrive in it, the outlaw leader must have been a very different man from the exemplary hero we see in most versions of his story. A ruthless, anti-hero Robin is in evidence in recent novels as different as Angus Donald's *Outlaw* and Adam Thorpe's *Hodd*.

Donald's blood-filled adventure novel, published in 2009, is narrated by Alan Dale, a teenage cutpurse in Nottingham, who joins Robin's band and begins a slow transformation into warrior minstrel. Most of the other traditional characters are present in the story, although often in slightly altered form. Little John is a foul-mouthed giant with a taste for elaborately blasphemous curses ('By God's hairy bollocks!') and sexual innuendo; Maid Marian is Marie-Anne, Countess of Locksley. Robin has a brother, Hugh, who has accompanied him to Sherwood and plays a central role in the plot of *Outlaw*. In providing Robin with an identity, Donald makes use of the long-established theory, first suggested in the nineteenth century, that the outlaw's real name was Odo. Robert Odo, or Robin Hood, in Donald's novel is a charismatic figure to whom narrator Alan is irresisistibly drawn but, for those brought up on kinder versions of the outlaw, his most distinctive characteristic is his capacity for cruelty and violence. He cuts out the tongue of an informer. He orders the limb-by-limb dismemberment of Sir John Peveril, a rival guerrilla leader who has trespassed on his territory. Friar Tuck tells Alan of an occasion when Robin cold-bloodedly initiated the slaughter of a group of priests. This is not the genial captain of the greenwood familiar from so many other tellings of the tales. Donald's Robin is contemptuous of Christian beliefs and a man drawn to the old gods but, again, his paganism is not the faintly New Age mysticism that can be found in, say, the *Robin of Sherwood* TV series. This Robin is comfortable with violent ritual and one of the more memorable scenes in the book shows him playing the horned god Cernunnos in a frenzied ceremony that culminates in a human sacrifice. Angus Donald has since written sequels to *Outlaw*. *Holy Warrior* has Alan Dale following his master Robert Odo, now pardoned by Richard the Lionheart, to the Holy Land and fights in the Third Crusade. *King's Man* records the outlaws' involvement in the ransoming of Richard from his imprisonment.

Hodd, first published in the same year as Donald's very different work, is a novel that plays sophisticated games with narrative and with ideas of history. (*Hodd* was not the first novel on the subject of Robin in which the author turned his back on conventional narrative. There is an interesting work from 1981 by Peter Vansittart entitled *The Death of Robin Hood* which moves backward and forward in time to show Robin as an archetypal figure in English history, his presence felt both in the medieval forest and in later social struggles such as the nineteenth-century Luddite riots.) The main body of Thorpe's book purports to be a manuscript that was discovered in a French church by a soldier during the First World War. In peace time the soldier was a Cambridge-educated scholar of medieval history and, after the war was finished, he retired to a small English village and translated the manuscript from Latin. This translation, complete with scholarly footnotes, is what we are supposed to be reading. The text itself is the work of an ancient monk, more than ninety years old in 1305, the year he picks up his quill, who is looking back to his youthful experience of meeting a strange, unpredictable and intermittently violent outlaw named Robert Hodd. In fact, the narrator turns out to be the familiar character Much (although he is not quite Much the Miller's Son as recorded in the ballads and later versions of the legend) and some of the events he relates echo the story told in 'Robin Hood and the Monk'.

The Robin of *Hodd* is a man of violence in a violent world. When the narrator, as a teenage boy with a gift for playing the harp, is captured by the outlaws, one of his fellow prisoners is a 'tregetour' or conjuror who annoys the gang's leader. The man is forced to climb a tree and is later pinned to one of its branches by an arrow through the hand. He dies a slow and painful death up in the forest canopy, the target of Hodd's cruel mockery as he does so. Later in the book, the outlaw mutilates and cuts the noses off other captives. Yet this Robin is also a strange and remarkable man. He is a heretic who denies the existence of God and sin and believes that he himself has attained a state of perfection in which he can do no wrong. (The fictional scholar who is providing a commentary on the manuscript suggests that Hodd's ideas are similar to those of the Brethren of the Free Spirit, a heretical group in early-thirteenth century Europe, and the outlaw later admits to having travelled on the continent as a young man.) Despite his fear of Hodd and his horror at his ideas, the narrator also finds himself drawn to the charismatic outlaw and he becomes, for a time, one of his followers. As a musician, he even composes songs celebrating his exploits and, in an ironic twist that unsettles his old age, these songs become the means by which Hodd's reputation grows in the decades after the outlaw's death.

In their different ways, the books by Angus Donald and Adam Thorpe both demonstrate how alive and how adaptable the Robin Hood legend remains. Writers of all kinds can continue to find inspiration in it. *Outlaw* shows that Robin can still form the basis for what is, beneath its gory modernity, a rather old-fashioned adventure story. *Hodd*, a work of great sophistication and linguistic ingenuity, and arguably the best novel about Robin to be published in the last fifty years, reveals the extent to which the old stories can be reworked by an imaginative and ambitious writer.

Robin on the Screen

Cinema

The very first Robin Hood films were produced before the First World War. In Britain, the pioneering director Percy Stow was responsible for over 200 shorts between 1904 and 1915, all made by the Clarendon Film Company which had studios in Croydon. One of these, made in 1908, was entitled *Robin Hood and His Merry Men*. Unfortunately the film does not survive and, since it was not common practice at the time to credit the actors in such movies, we have no way of knowing the name of the man who first played Robin Hood on screen. Judging by a brief summary in the trade press at the time, Stow followed what had become, by the early years of the twentieth century, the standard narrative for the outlaw by making him a dispossessed nobleman in search of justice. In the USA, *Robin Hood* of 1912 was a thirty-minute-long film, starring Robert Frazer, an actor who was still active more than three decades later, appearing in low-budget Westerns and cheap serials well into the 1940s. Made in Fort Lee, New Jersey, then one of the centres of American filmmaking, the movie still survives and has been given public screenings several times in the last few years. The plot focuses on Robin's rivalry with both the Sheriff of Nottingham and Sir Guy of Gisbourne but the film is perhaps most notable for its curious use of special effects. Years before Disney animators decided that Robin was a fox and the Sheriff a wolf, the makers of this silent chose to illustrate a character's nature by briefly fading to a shot of an animal when he or she first appeared. In 1912, another American company, the Thanhouser Film Corporation, produced *Robin Hood and Maid Marian* starring William Russell and Gerda Holmes in the title roles, which can probably claim to be the first film about the outlaw to be turned into a novel. The following year *The Pluck Library*, a British boys' weekly which regularly advertised its 'Stories from the Cinema', published a seven-part adaptation of the movie written by William Murray Graydon, a prolific author of such adventure fiction.

All of these were only the forerunners for what was to be the first great Robin Hood film – the 1922 version starring Douglas Fairbanks. The actor was then at the height of his success and, in films such as *The Mark of Zorro* (1920) and *The Three Musketeers* (1921), had demonstrated a talent for athletic swashbuckling that had made him one of the biggest stars of the day. He was looking for another historical costume role and Robin Hood might have appeared an ideal choice. In fact, Fairbanks was initially reluctant to play what he called 'a flat-footed Englishman walking through the woods' but he was soon persuaded that the part could be tailored for his particular brand of energetic heroism. Vast sums were spent on creating a huge castle set and a reconstruction of twelfth-century Nottingham in the Pickford-Fairbanks Studio in Hollywood and Allan Dwan, who had worked with Fairbanks's wife Mary Pickford on several pictures, was hired as director. The film premiered at the recently built Grauman's Egyptian Theatre on Hollywood Boulevard in October 1922. Reviewers liked it and it became one of the big commercial hits of the year. The film divides neatly into two halves. For its first hour, an idle viewer, chancing on the movie without seeing the opening titles, might be forgiven for not realising that it is about Robin Hood at all. The focus is on Richard the Lionheart, presiding over a great tournament before he departs for the Crusades, and on the champion jouster, the Earl of Huntingdon, winning the tournament prize and becoming the bashful target for the admiring attention of the court ladies, including the Lady Marian Fitzwalter. The names might alert the knowledgeable to the fact that this is a Robin Hood film but otherwise it simply seems like a hugely ambitious reconstruction of what silent-era Hollywood imagined medieval England to be.

It is only in the second half of the film, with the Earl of Huntingdon exiled to Sherwood through the machinations of Prince John and Sir Guy of Gisbourne, that some of the more familiar Robin Hood motifs (although, even now, not as many of them as might be expected) begin to appear. The vast sets, which Fairbanks had earlier worried would dwarf him, become a giant playground for his acrobatics. No Robin Hood in cinematic history, not even Errol Flynn, has moved with the grace and energy he does. He races around the castle battlements, sending the Sheriff of Nottingham's soldiers skittling as he does so; he abseils down an enormous curtain that has been conveniently hung in one of the castle's loftier rooms; he uses a descending drawbridge as his personal climbing-frame. In the climactic scenes, Robin's men invade Nottingham Castle in huge hordes (he seems to have gathered half the country's male population in the greenwood) and comprehensively thwart the villains' plans. Ninety years on, Fairbanks's *Robin Hood* remains one of the most significant of all films to be made about the legendary outlaw. Many of what are now the most familiar features of Robin Hood on screen may be missing from it but, to a large extent, it defined the Hollywood 'swashbuckler' genre and created a template for screen stories of Robin that was influential for decades to come.

So successful was the Fairbanks movie that it deterred other filmmakers from attempting to put the Robin Hood story on the screen. How could they match the scale and spectacle of the 1922 film? During the rest of the silent era and the first ten years of the 'talkies', there were only two Robin Hood films made in the US and Britain, both of them now very obscure indeed. *Robin Hood Junior* from 1923 was an American movie, starring a then popular child actor named Frankie Lee in the role of the outlaw as a boy. *The Merry Men of Sherwood* was a thirty-minute short, now lost, produced in 1932 by a maverick English director with the delightfully ludicrous name of Widgey Newman. This neglect of the Robin Hood story was to end in 1938 with the release of the Technicolor Warner Bros movie *The Adventures of Robin Hood*, starring Errol Flynn. Difficult as it is to credit now, the role was originally intended for James Cagney, one of Warners' biggest stars at the time, but commonsense prevailed and the part eventually went to Flynn, already a successful swashbuckler in films like *Captain Blood* and *The Charge of the Light Brigade*. The original director was William Keighley but, when Keighley fell behind schedule and out of favour, he was replaced by Michael Curtiz who had directed Flynn in both of those films.

More than seventy years after it was made, *The Adventures of Robin Hood* remains the archetypal, swashbuckling screen version of the story. There are other films which are more self-consciously realistic in their reconstruction of the medieval past. There are other re-tellings which work harder to bring out the continuing relevance of the legend to the present day. However, there is no version which is as richly colourful, as energetic and lively, as fast-moving and romantic. In short, there is no screen Robin Hood which is as much *fun* as the Flynn film. Flynn himself is exactly right for the part. At the height of his physical charisma, before years of indulgence bloated and coarsened him, he is a brilliant embodiment of Robin as both a fighter for justice and a trickster of the greenwood. He is supported by a brilliant cast of regular Warner players, from Olivia de Havilland as his Maid Marian and Basil Rathbone as a forcefully villainous Sir Guy of Gisbourne to Claude Rains as wicked Prince John and Alan Hale, repeating his role as Little John from the Fairbanks film twenty years earlier.

The plot is founded on the Saxon v. Norman conflict that dates back to Scott and the audience is thrust into it from the very first scenes in which Robin saves Much the Miller's Son after the latter has poached one of the king's deer. Robin himself, however, is the gentrified Robin, a Saxon noble who believes in fair play and tolerance. 'It's injustice I hate,' he says, 'not the Normans.' The filmmakers find space for many of the most familiar set-pieces from literary sources (the confrontation on the log bridge between Robin and Little John, Robin's first meeting with the Curtal Friar/Friar Tuck) and they create memorable versions of them. They also introduce new scenes which have an instant impact. After first seeing it, who can forget Robin's entrance into Prince John's court, strutting into the room with a cocky grin on his face and a deer across his shoulders which he hurls onto the dining table? Or the carnivalesque feast in the forest at which Robin and his men entertain a reluctant Sir Guy, and the outlaw leader shows Marian the realities of Saxon poverty which her sheltered Norman upbringing has hidden from her? *The Adventures of Robin Hood* is both a brilliant embodiment of earlier motifs from the legends and the source for new ideas about them which echo down the decades since it was made.

In the forties, almost any film where the plot focused on a noble thief who stole from the rich and gave to the poor was likely to be given a Robin Hood title in the hope that it would be able to bask in the reflected glory of the still-popular Flynn film. Thus we have *Robin Hood of the Pecos* in 1941, *Robin Hood of the Range* in 1943 and both *Robin Hood of Texas* and *Robin Hood of Monterey* in 1947. None had anything to do with the English outlaw hero; nearly all were Westerns. However, there were two movies in that decade that dared to be compared with Warners' brilliant swashbuckler even if neither could hope to come close to matching its mix of wit and action-packed entertainment. Both of them emerged from the studios of Columbia Pictures. In *The Bandit of Sherwood Forest* from 1946, Cornel Wilde is a poor man's Errol Flynn as Robert of Nottingham, son of the original Sherwood outlaw (Russell Hicks), who gathers together his father's ageing comrades to fight new injustices when England's ancient liberties are threatened by a greedy Regent. An attempt to reprise the success of the earlier film on a fraction of its budget, *The Bandit of Sherwood Forest* soon loses its way and ends up as no more than a competent and mildly enjoyable variant of the story. As is often the case in such movies, the villains are given more chance to impress themselves on the memory than the heroes. Henry Daniell is sneeringly malevolent as the Regent and he is ably assisted by George Macready as his accomplice in plotting treason. Robert of Nottingham and his merry men seem a bit pallid in comparison, although Wilde, as a former fencing champion, makes the most of his opportunities to cross swords with his foes. Two years later Columbia released *The Prince of Thieves*, starring Jon Hall, an actor largely forgotten now but familiar at the time from Technicolor Arabian Nights romances such as *Ali Baba and the Forty Thieves*. As Robin, Hall occasionally looks the part but he lacks any real acting talent and the story into which the scriptwriters thrust him – a dull variant of the ballad tale of the outlaws helping a young man to rescue his true love from the clutches of a rival suitor – gives him little chance to shine.

Like *The Bandit of Sherwood Forest*, *Rogues of Sherwood Forest* (1950), also a Columbia production, is an attempt to create a new Robin Hood story by focusing on the outlaw's son. If Cornel Wilde, in the earlier film, is a poor man's Errol Flynn, then the star of this movie, John Derek (future husband of Ursula Andress and Bo Derek), is a poor man's Cornel Wilde who has nothing much to recommend him beyond his improbable good looks. The charisma-free Derek plays Robin, Earl of Huntington who reforms his father's band of merry men to combat the oppression of King John, played by George Macready. Diana Lynn in the Maid Marian role, a ward of the king who becomes Robin's spy at court, is as colourless as her lover. In his last role, Alan Hale, who had played the part opposite Douglas Fairbanks in 1922 and Errol Flynn in 1938, is Little John, although his presence does little more than remind viewers of how much better those earlier films were than the one they are currently watching. Plump vaudevillian Billy House is well cast as Friar Tuck; one-time silent comedian Billy Bevan plays Will Scarlett; Paul Cavanagh enjoys himself as Sir Giles, the king's villainous sidekick. The plot culminates in a version of the signing of the Magna Carta that never made it into the history books.

Two further Robin films followed in quick succession. *Tales of Robin Hood*, a pilot for a TV series that was never made, was released as a B-movie in 1951. The outlaw leader was played by Robert Clarke who went on to become the star of low-budget SF films with titles like *The Astounding She-Monster* and *The Hideous Sun Demon*. Cheap and cheerful, the film has few pretensions but, within the huge limitations imposed on it by shortage of cash, it tells its tales quite well. The following year Disney turned its attention to the outlaw of Sherwood and the result was *The Story of Robin Hood and His Merrie Men*. Few of the budgetary constraints that affected *Tales of Robin Hood* applied to the Disney Studios and, on paper at least, the movie had a lot going for it. The strong cast was headed by Richard Todd as Robin, Peter Finch as the Sheriff of Nottingham and the suitably hulking James Robertson Justice as Little John. It was directed by Ken Annakin who made a number of live-action feature films for Disney including *The Sword and the Rose* (also starring Todd) and *Swiss Family Robinson*. Much of it was shot on location in the English countryside. And yet somehow *The Story of Robin Hood and His Merrie Men* doesn't quite work. Todd, who was to become best known for stiff-upper-lip roles in war movies like *The Dambusters*, looks uncomfortable in Lincoln Green and rarely exudes the charm and confidence required to carry off the part. The script makes extensive use of familiar stories (the initial confrontation between Robin and Little John is particularly well done) but it never really comes together to form a coherent narrative. In one sense, the filmmakers are too reverential towards the old legend. *The Story of Robin Hood and His Merrie Men* might have been a better film had they been prepared to trust their own imaginations a little more. Instead, it feels too familiar and too staid an interpretation.

After this Disney version, Hollywood in the fifties and sixties showed no further interest in the Robin Hood stories. In Britain, *Son of Robin Hood* was released in 1958, a curiously titled film since the son turns out to be a daughter, played by June Laverick. Directed by the imported American George Sherman, a specialist in Westerns, this was a re-run of the idea that Robin's former merry men are brought together again by a chip off the old block, with the added variant that, in this instance, Hood Junior is a girl. Described by one film historian as 'cheaply produced, appallingly written and woefully acted', *Son of Robin Hood* has very little to recommend it. It was left to Hammer Film Productions, best known for their Dracula and Frankenstein films, to put halfway decent versions of the story onto the larger screens.

Over a period of nearly twenty years, Hammer was responsible for no less than four Robin Hood movies. The first of these was *The Men of Sherwood Forest* (1954), directed by Val Guest and starring Don Taylor, an American actor who moved behind the camera twenty years later and was in the director's chair for a number of films in the seventies and eighties including *Escape from the Planet of the Apes* and *The Island of Dr. Moreau*. Notable as the first film Hammer produced in colour, this in an intriguing Robin movie, if only because it makes little attempt to re-tell the familiar stories from the legend but instead focuses on a single, new narrative. The plot, focusing on an attempt by a villain called Sir Guy (but not of Gisbourne) to assassinate Richard the Lionheart, is neatly constructed and a welcome change from the often episodic nature of other Robin films. As the hero, Taylor shows why his change of career from actor to director was a wise one and is rarely more than adequate but he has sterling support from a number of familiar British character actors of the period. Reginald Beckwith is particularly effective as Friar Tuck. *Sword of Sherwood Forest*, which was released in 1961, was an attempt to cash in on the success of the ITV series starring Richard Greene as the outlaw. By the time this moderately enjoyable swash-buckler was made, Greene had been playing Robin Hood so long he could take on the role in his sleep and there are times in the movie when he appears to be doing exactly that. A miscast Peter Cushing seems only half-heartedly villainous as the Sheriff of Nottingham and the scriptwriter hastens him out of the plot before its conclusion, replacing him as chief baddie with the Earl of Newark, played by Richard Pasco. Nigel Green makes an effective enough Little John but Niall MacGinnis is a poor Friar Tuck and Sarah Branch, an actress who appeared in only a handful of films in the late fifties and early sixties, is out of her depth as Maid Marian. In supporting roles, Jack Gwillim plays a fighting archbishop, as eager for a bout of swordplay as he is for a religious service, and a young Oliver Reed is a camply menacing sidekick to the wicked Earl. The unnecessarily complicated plot involves a fatally wounded man with a dying message of danger to deliver, the Sheriff's attempts to confiscate land when the true owner dies in the Crusades and a conspiracy to assassinate the archbishop. Greene as Robin strides through it as if he's seen it all before and can hardly wait for the climactic swordfight in which the good will triumph and the bad will meet a sticky end.

At the time Hammer made *A Challenge for Robin Hood* in 1967, some of the energy and inventiveness that had characterised the company in the fifties and early sixties was beginning to dissipate. Their horror films were losing their vigour and, on the evidence of this Robin movie, so too were their historical swashbucklers. *A Challenge for Robin Hood* is a much poorer film than either *The Men of Sherwood Forest* or *The Sword of Sherwood Forest*. The plot, which has Robin as a Norman lord falsely accused of murder who flees to the forest and takes over the leadership of the band of outlaws there, is dull and predictable. The action sequences are leaden and unconvincing. The actors playing the Merry Men look distinctly unhappy. Only James Hayter as Friar Tuck, reprising the role he had taken in the 1952 Disney film, looks as if he is enjoying himself. By far the biggest problem with the film, however, is the casting of Barrie Ingham as Robin. Ingham has had a long and successful career in the theatre and he holds the distinction of being one of the few actors to have played roles in both *Dr. Who* and *Star Trek* but nature never intended him to play Robin Hood. Not to mince words, he looks and sounds ridiculous as the hero of the greenwood. Thirty-three at the time the film was made, he appears older and he has been equipped with one of the most unflattering medieval hairstyles ever to hit the silver screen. Combine these disadvantages with a voice seemingly more suitable for drawing-room comedy than the wilds of Sherwood Forest and we have a Robin memorable for all the wrong reasons.

Wolfshead: The Legend of Robin Hood, the last of the Hammer Robin movies, was originally made in 1969 as a pilot episode for a proposed series on London Weekend Television. The TV company decided not to go ahead with the series and the pilot looked likely never to gain an audience until, several years later, Hammer bought it and gave it a theatrical release as the lower half of a double bill. Only an hour long and with a familiar enough plot in which Robin the honest Saxon is outlawed by a wicked Norman lord and forced to fight back, this is not, in most ways, a major addition to the canon of Robin Hood movies. Narrative coherence has been lost in the transformation from TV pilot to cinematic second feature and the film is clearly not a self-contained story but the first in what was originally planned as a series of episodes. Lady Marian would doubtless have had more to do had the series been commissioned but, in the film we have, she seems superfluous to requirements. However, there is much of interest in *Wolfshead*. Seen in the context of the history of Robin Hood on screen, it is the first film to move entirely away from the romantic swashbuckling tradition of Fairbanks and Flynn and strive instead for some degree of realism. It is interesting to speculate about the possible success of the series had it been made. Would 1969 have been a good year in which to launch a realistic Robin Hood TV series? In fact, as we shall see, there was no series on the small screen featuring the outlaw leader between the end of the nineteen fifties and the middle of the nineteen seventies. David Warbeck, who played Robin in *Wolfshead*, would have made an interestingly brooding hero in any ongoing series but fate had another path in store for him. He went on to become a regular performer in cult Italian horror films of the 1980s.

It was not just in Britain and the USA that Robin Hood movies were made. As far back as the silent era a Japanese film entitled *Robin Hood No Yume* was produced. More recently, there have been movies from Holland (*Robin Hood en Zijn Schelmen*, 1962), from Brazil (*Robin Hood, O Trapalhão da Floresta*, 1974), from Spain (*Robin Hood Nunca Muere*, 1975) and from Russia (*Strely Robin Guda*, 1975). However, during much the same period that Hammer was making its Robin Hood films in Britain, the country that was producing the most versions of the outlaw's story was Italy. By the late fifties, the Italian film industry already had a rich tradition of costume drama and swashbucklers so it was perhaps no surprise that its movie-makers regularly turned their attentions to the subject of Robin and his merry men, although the results were decidedly mixed. One-time Tarzan Lex Barker played the outlaw in *Robin Hood e I Pirati* (*Robin Hood and the Pirates*) in 1960, an unlikely story in which Robin joins forces with a band of shipwrecked buccaneers to fight against a villain who has killed his father. *Il Trionfo di Robin Hood* (*The Triumph of Robin Hood*) was released two years later. Starring the Scottish actor Don Burnett in the title role, it was directed by Umberto Lenzi, later notorious for exploitation films such as *Cannibal Ferox*, one of the movies condemned as 'video nasties' in the 1980s. Lenzi's film is a more traditional telling of the tale than *Robin Hood and the Pirates* and features most of the familiar Sherwood characters in a story involving attempts to ransom Richard the Lionheart from imprisonment in Europe. *Il Magnifico Robin Hood*, from 1970, was an Italian-Spanish co-production and starred a Spanish actor Francisco Martinez Celeiro, billed under the more Anglo-Saxon sounding alias of George Martin. The best of these Italian films is undoubtedly *L'Arciere di Sherwood* from 1971 which has Giuliano Gemma, better known as the star of spaghetti westerns, in the title role. Flashing improbably gleaming smiles for the Middle Ages, Gemma and Mark Damon, the American actor who plays an Allen-a-Dale given a higher profile than in other films, take on the assorted baddies with some gusto. The movie, unfathomably called *The Scalawag Bunch* in its only release in English, is a lively swashbuckler which adds little new to Robin's cinematic history but entertainingly revisits some familiar scenes (the archery contest, Richard the Lionheart's incognito return to England) from earlier films.

L'Arciere di Sherwood must have seemed old-fashioned even at the time of its release. The most thoroughgoing attempt in the seventies to give a new twist to the story, however, was fated to be a commercial failure. What happens to legends when they grow old? That is the question asked by Richard Lester's 1976 film *Robin and Marian*, arguably the most unusual and the most affecting of all the many movies made about the outlaw leader.

Other cinematic Robins tend to live in a fantasy world of swashbuckling heroism and perpetual youth. In Lester's touching and beautifully acted film, he inhabits the real world in which time passes and men and women grow old. Sean Connery's Robin Hood is no longer the dashing hero of the greenwood that he once was. He is middle-aged and beginning to feel his years in his aching joints and weary muscles. As the film opens, he and Little John, played by Nicol Williamson, are fighting with Richard the Lionheart (Richard Harris) in the Holy Land. Richard, in other films the epitome of the 'good king', is here shown as little more than a bloodthirsty tyrant and the two men have grown tired of giving their loyalty to a man who has no qualms about butchering men, women and children if they stand in his way. When the king is killed, they decide to return home to England. They have been absent for twenty years. Maid Marian (Audrey Hepburn in one of the best performances of her later career) has long been the abbess of a priory near Nottingham but Robin's return reignites the old love between them. She joins him in Sherwood once again. Meanwhile, Robin's old enemy, the Sheriff of Nottingham, brilliantly played by Robert Shaw not as a villain but as a humane and intelligent man who recognises how much he and the old outlaw leader have in common, is still around to continue their feud. When Robin gathers a new band of men in Sherwood, everyone but him recognises that the days of swashbuckling heroism are gone. As the outlaws battle once again with the Sheriff's men and Robin faces a bruising and bloody encounter with his old rival, even he realises that his time has passed. *Robin and Marian* becomes one of the very few films to depict the death of Robin Hood. James Goldman's script for the movie and Lester's direction include some of the comic, almost slapstick, touches that enlivened the latter's Three Musketeers films but the prevailing feeling is one of melancholy and regret at the departure of youth and romance.

Robin Hood

For all its many virtues, *Robin and Marian* was something of a flop at the box office. In fact, it is rumoured to have been the only Robin Hood film ever to lose money. Perhaps partly as a consequence of this, although the eighties saw the success on TV of *Robin of Sherwood*, it was not until the early nineties that the outlaw leader returned to the big screen. Unfortunately, when he did, it was Kevin Costner who played him. The 1991 film *Robin Hood: Prince of Thieves* has its good points and it remains a movie that is entertaining enough to watch. As it opens, Robert of Locksley is languishing in a Saracen dungeon in Jerusalem. With the assistance of a Moorish fellow-prisoner, played with his usual gravitas by Morgan Freeman, he escapes and makes his way back to England. Things have not been going well in his absence. His father has been killed by the Sheriff and his lands confiscated. Before he has the chance to say Jack Robinson, our hero is exiled to Sherwood Forest where he encounters a motley crew of outlaws who are skulking in its depths. Displaying both natural leadership skills and an obtrusive American accent he seems to have acquired during his years of imprisonment, Locksley inspires them to rise above the petty thievery they've been indulging in for years and to dream of freedom and the defeat of their enemies, principally (of course) the Sheriff of Nottingham. They steal the money the Sheriff has been gathering to bribe the barons of England into joining him in rebellion against Richard the Lionheart. The Sheriff retaliates by burning their forest community to the ground and taking some of their comrades to hang in Nottingham but Locksley, now the legend known as Robin Hood, organises a daring raid on the town. The men are rescued. So too is Mary Elizabeth Mastrantonio's Lady Marian, cousin to the King, whom the Sheriff is forcing into marriage as part of his plans to seize the throne. As the Sheriff, magnificently over the top in his pantomime villainy, Alan Rickman steals the show. Mannered and menacing, threatening to cut out Robin's heart with a spoon rather than an axe because 'it'll hurt more', Rickman's Sheriff seems to be appearing in an entirely different (probably better) film than the one through which Costner's Robin is heroically striding. *Robin Hood: Prince of Thieves* is often rousingly energetic in its action (the final duel between hero and villain is very well staged) but it is too long and meandering, and too sentimental to be a particularly good version of the legend. Most damningly of all, Costner is completely wrong in the central role. At his best as an actor when playing an American everyman such as the hero of *Field of Dreams*, he looks lost and ever so slightly ludicrous as Robin Hood.

By chance, the same year, 1991, saw the release in the UK and Europe of a better Robin film that was sadly overshadowed by the Costner version. *Robin Hood*, originally shown as a TV movie in the USA, starred Patrick Bergin in the title role and a young Uma Thurman as Maid Marian. Taking the familiar Saxons versus Normans rivalry as its focus but introducing a new villain in the shape of Sir Miles Folcanet (played by the German actor Jürgen Prochnow), the film has a kind of gritty authenticity that is noticeably absent from *Prince of Thieves*. Sherwood is not the sunlight-dappled never-never land in which Costner makes his impassioned, unconvincing orations in favour of freedom but a dark and dank forest in which medieval outlaws might well lurk. Bergin, although he is sporting an extremely unfortunate moustache, makes Robin a far more compelling and ambivalent figure than Costner's improbably all-American hero, and Thurman, moving from coquettish spoilt brat to strong and resourceful woman in the course of the film, is excellent as Marian. It is just a pity that, whereas Costner's film is and always has been readily watchable, this *Robin Hood* has rarely found an audience.

In the two decades and more since Costner and Bergin entered the greenwood, Robin has appeared onscreen in a variety of incarnations, none of them very impressive. The 2001 made-for-

TV movie, *Princess of Thieves*, had Robin (Stuart Wilson) as bad father to daughter Gwyn (Keira Knightley), absent at the Crusades during her crucial formative years and all too willing to dismiss her wish to fight against wicked Prince John, simply on the grounds that she is a woman. Gwyn proceeds to cut her hair and don male garb in order to help Richard the Lionheart's illegitimate son Philip seize power from John in a *coup d'etat* otherwise unknown to history. Robin's daughter proves herself as brilliant an archer as her father in yet another screen version of the famous archery tournament won when one arrow splits another in the bullseye. She also engages in a coy romance with the young prince after he spots that she's not quite the boy she claims to be. *Robin Hood: Prince of Sherwood* (2008) is an embarrassingly inept and amateurish straight-to-video confection. It was made in Alabama and it shows. *Beyond Sherwood Forest*, another made-for-TV movie from 2009 proved a misguided attempt to fuse the Robin Hood stories with the sword and sorcery genre. Directed by Peter DeLuise, the son of Mel Brooks regular Dom DeLuise who appeared in *Robin Hood: Men in Tights*, it starred the Canadian actor Robin Dunne in the lead role. An uninspired CGI dragon shape-shifting into a naked woman and a gateway in the deep woods to an alternative world prove inadequate substitutes for an interesting script and a truly original take on the legend. The best that can be said of the film is that it shows how open the Robin Hood myth is to endless reinterpretations, even ones as misguided as this is.

The most expensive, ambitious and eagerly-anticipated Robin movie of recent years, however, has been Ridley Scott's take on the story, released in 2010. Starring Russell Crowe as a character named, for no particularly good reason, Robin Longstride, *Robin Hood* also features Cate Blanchett as an independent and spirited Lady Marian. The whole film is an 'origins tale', describing how Robin took to the woods and became an outlaw. Many of the literary versions of the story have provided such an explanatory opening but they don't usually extend to more than a chapter. This tale lasts close on two and a half hours. Robin fights in the armies of Richard the Lionheart and is present when the king dies while besieging a castle in France. Heading back home to England, he and his pals (a Welsh Will Scarlet, Alan A'Dayle and Little John) witness the ambush and murder of the knights bearing news of Richard's death to London. They take the place of these knights, one of whom is Sir Robert Loxley. Masquerading as Loxley, Robin travels to the dead man's home near Nottingham and is persuaded by Sir Robert's father to continue his pretence. Warily, he does so and is welcomed back as the prodigal son and long-lost husband of the Lady Marian. As wicked King John squeezes the northern barons for tax monies they have not got and Philip of France, assisted by a traitor in English ranks, plots to invade, Robin becomes a leader of the resistance to tyranny of all kinds. He and the other northern noblemen make an alliance with John to defeat the perfidious French but, once they have won their victory, the king goes back on his word. Robin is proclaimed an outlaw. He and Marian and his comrades retire to the greenwood. The very last shot before the credits roll is of a title card, reading 'And so the legend begins.'

Ridley Scott and his principal writer Brian Helgeland have thus turned their backs entirely on the traditional stories and fashioned an entirely new narrative about the outlaw hero. Unfortunately, it isn't a particularly compelling or engaging one. Indeed, there are times when it seems to have little to do with Robin Hood at all. It could be any kind of lavish exercise in Hollywood medieval. The connection with the character of folklore sometimes appears slender indeed. This is certainly the most spectacular Robin Hood film since the Fairbanks and Flynn versions but it lacks most of the grace and fluency of those two movies. Like its star, who has a tendency to take himself very seriously indeed, it has little lightness of spirit. It is a ponderous film, filled with grunting action sequences and Crowe's embarrassingly banal and anachronistic speeches about life, liberty and the Saxon pursuit of happiness. However, Ridley Scott's *Robin Hood* has been a box office success, despite its huge cost, and it has at least established Robin as once again a suitable hero for the big screen. There have been rumours that Scott himself might produce a sequel. This may seem unlikely, given that the director has never had a second bite at any movie cherry and has always moved on to new projects, but the ending of the first film certainly seems to suggest that others could be in the pipeline. What is almost certainly true is that Robin will continue to make his mark in the cinema.

TV

The very first person to play Robin Hood on British TV was the future Dr. Who, Patrick Troughton, who took the role in a six-part BBC series in 1953. Unfortunately it is almost impossible to judge how good or bad he was in the part because only one episode has been preserved and that one episode is very rarely seen. Troughton proved, however, to be merely trailblazing a path through Sherwood that was to be followed by one of the best-remembered and best-loved of all Robin Hoods to appear on either large or small screen.

In 1954, legendary British media mogul Lew Grade joined forces with the American producer Hannah Weinstein to finance a series of half-hour shows about the outlaw to be shown on the newly-launched ITV network in Britain and on CBS in the United States. The actor chosen for the title role in *The Adventures of Robin Hood* was Richard Greene. Greene was born in Plymouth, a member of a family that had been producing stage actors for generations, and was only twenty when his talent and good looks won him a contract with Twentieth Century Fox. He appeared in a number of Hollywood films (perhaps most famously, he played Sir Henry Baskerville in *The Hound of the Baskervilles*, the 1939 movie that first paired together Basil Rathbone and Nigel Bruce as Sherlock Holmes and Dr. Watson) but the Second World War, in which he served as a British army officer, effectively put an end to his hopes of major stardom. His career was languishing in the doldrums of second-rate swashbucklers like *The Bandits of Corsica* and *Captain Scarlett* when he was approached to play Robin Hood. He went on to become identified with the role in a way that few other actors have ever been.

For its time, *The Adventures of Robin Hood*, first screened on British TV in September 1955, was clever popular entertainment and it remains very watchable. In the opening episode, Robin is the returning crusader forced into outlawry by the machinations of his Norman enemies but, as the series progressed, the circumstances which led him to Sherwood are almost forgotten. He and his usual gang are just there, ready at a moment's notice to sally forth to right injustice and put the Sheriff's nose out of joint. Greene plays Robin as an almost avuncular character, more dependable than dashing, but he also gives him real presence and personality. The regular supporting cast of Archie Duncan as a surprisingly Scottish Little John, Alexander Gauge as Friar Tuck and Bernadette O'Farrell (in the first two series) and Patricia Driscoll (in the last two) as Maid Marian all seem at ease with their characters. Many of the actors who appeared occasionally in the series went on to greater renown. Screening successive episodes today can become an enjoyable exercise in spotting the famous face. Both Steptoe and Son (Wilfred Brambell and Harry H. Corbett) were in the series more than once, although never in the same episode; Sid James, in pre-Carry On days, played a master silversmith; Donald Pleasence took the role of Prince John on four occasions; Leslie Phillips had several different roles; Jane Asher appeared as a child actress; Leo McKern, Rumpole of the Bailey many years in the future, played a villainous knight named Sir Roger DeLisle in the very first episode. Some of the directors were men of real talent. Terence Fisher, who directed eleven episodes in the first series, was soon to gain fame for his work on Hammer horror classics such as *The Curse of Frankenstein* and *Dracula*; Lindsay Anderson directed five later episodes, although it would be a struggle to find much evidence in them of the sensibility of the future *auteur* who created revolutionary British films like *If* and *O Lucky Man!*; Bernard Knowles was a former cinematographer who had frequently worked with Hitchcock; and Don Chaffey went on to direct Hammer kitsch classics *One Million Years BC* and *Creatures the World Forgot*.

However, in many ways, the most interesting participants in the series were the writers. Look in reference works or on websites such as the Internet Movie Database and the scriptwriters for *The Adventures of Robin Hood* very often seem to be people with few other credits. The reason is simple. Most of the credited names were either aliases or fronts. The real writers were American screenwriters who had been blacklisted in Hollywood after falling foul of the notorious, McCarthyite campaign against former Communists in the film industry. Howard Koch, who contributed scripts with his wife under the name of 'Anne Rodney', had worked with Orson Welles on the legendary radio adaptation of HG Wells's *The War of the Worlds* which had sent tens of thousands of Americans into panic-stricken flight across the country. He was also one of the writers of *Casablanca*, the 1941 Humphrey Bogart classic. Ring Lardner Jr, who wrote episodes from the beginning as 'Eric Heath', was one of the so-called 'Hollywood Ten' jailed for resisting demands to answer the questions of the House Un-American Activities Committee about their past political involvement. Waldo Salt, later an Oscar winner for his script for *Midnight Cowboy*, who endured many years in the Hollywood wilderness after refusing to testify to the committee, wrote episodes as 'Arthur Behr'. Thus many of the stories of the famous English outlaw were written by Americans who had themselves been outlawed from working in their own country. In these circumstances, it is no surprise that the plots in the TV series keep returning again and again to themes of betrayal and treachery.

For more than twenty years after the last of the 143 episodes of *The Adventures of Robin Hood* was broadcast in March 1959, it had no major TV successor, although ITV continued to show repeats throughout the early sixties. *The Legend of Robin Hood* from 1975 has its merits and its fans. Following a consecutive narrative across six episodes rather than having separate, largely self-contained tales proved an interesting innovation. Diane Keen makes a good Maid Marian and Paul Darrow, later famous as Avon in the BBC cult science fiction series *Blake's 7*, plays the Sheriff with some panache. However, few would claim it as TV's finest version of the legend. Martin Potter makes a stilted and uncharismatic Robin and the series now seems creaky and desperately old-fashioned. In some ways, it was too respectful of both the real history of the late twelfth century and of the traditional stories. What was needed to revitalise and reinvent Robin for TV audiences was a series that was unafraid of turning its back on conventional ways of portraying him. *Robin of Sherwood*, when it arrived nine years later, did exactly that.

The aim of Richard Carpenter, the creator and most regular writer of the series, was to reinvigorate the tradition for a new generation and fuse it with other myths of the English greenwood such as Herne the Hunter. The horned Herne becomes mentor to Michael Praed's Robin in the first episode and he continues to emerge regularly from the mist-shrouded trees to help the hero throughout the series. Robin becomes Herne's adopted son. It is telling that 'Sherwood' appears in the very title of the series since the forest plays as significant a role in it as any of the humans who inhabit it. Sherwood is not only a place of comfort and safety for the outlaws, it is also a place of magic and enchantment. It is the setting for pagan rituals overseen by Herne, antlered and clad in shaggy skins, and an arena in which the old gods and the old ways can be celebrated. Sorcery and the supernatural are deeply woven into the series' overarching narrative of the struggle between good and evil. In that same first episode in which Herne adopts the outlaw leader, Robin's principal antagonist is not so much Sir Guy of Gisbourne or the Sheriff of Nottingham but the Baron de Belleme, a master of the black arts. Slain by Robin at the end of that first episode, the Baron returns later, brought back from the dead by one of his witch-like handmaidens who puts the outlaw leader under a powerfully malign enchantment. As the series progressed, Carpenter continued to up the stakes in the primal confrontation he placed at its core. The two-part episode 'The Swords of Wayland' has Robin coming face to face with the Devil himself, conjured up by a powerful abbess, played by Rula Lenska, who has gone over to the dark side. Even Lucifer proves no match for the greenwood hero. Only death itself can down him and this comes at the end of the second series when the Sheriff's soldiers surround him and he chooses to sacrifice himself in the hope that Marian and Much will escape. And yet, if even Robin cannot quite survive death, he can at least be resurrected. In the third and final series, Robin of Loxley is no more but his place is taken by Robert, son of the Earl of Huntington, played by Jason Connery. Cleverly making use of both the earlier tradition that Robin was a yeoman and his later gentrification by writers like Anthony Munday, Carpenter has his hero first as man of the people and second as exiled nobleman.

According to taste, the mysticism and the myth-making in *Robin of Sherwood* probably make or mar the series. Yet they are not all that fuel the narrative. Inextricably linked with them is a strong awareness of the injustices and inequities of the society in which his hero operates. Carpenter's Robin is not just Herne's champion in a struggle against spiritual evil; he is also a crusader for the poor and the dispossessed, for all those scorned by the oppressive regime of the Sheriff of Nottingham. Within the constraints imposed by making a primetime TV show, *Robin of Sherwood* is a gritty, authentic portrayal of medieval life. The series is also full of innovatory twists and additions to the story. Not the least of them is the character of Nasir, played by Mark Ryan, a Saracen swordsman who appears in the first episode as the enchanted servant of de Belleme. After Robin kills de Belleme, Nasir is released from the spell under which he had been placed and decides to join the outlaws in Sherwood. The Muslim Merry Man, or indeed Woman, has since become a regular feature of recent re-tellings of the story. In the 1991 film *Robin Hood: Prince of Thieves*, Morgan Freeman plays the almost impossibly wise Moor named Azeem who accompanies Kevin Costner's Robin on his return from the Holy Land to England; in the BBC TV series which began in 2006, Anjali Jay is Djaq, the rescued Saracen slave who dresses as a boy and joins the gang in the greenwood.

In conclusion, although the series has its faults, *Robin of Sherwood* remains one of the greatest of all screen presentations of the legend. More than a quarter of a century after the last episodes were made, its influence lives on. Fan clubs flourish and conventions gather. Websites devoted to it proliferate. The occasional rumour that another series (or a one-off film) is to be made still emerges, only to be quashed. It seems likely that it will continue to be remembered with affection for decades to come.

Any admirer of the more traditional screen presentations of the outlaw who had been irritated by the mysticism of *Robin of Sherwood* would have been thrown into an apoplexy by *The New Adventures of Robin Hood*, a Franco-American production which ran for four seasons on Turner Network Television in 1997 and 1998. Starring Matthew Porretta as the hero in the first two series and John Bradley in the role for the last two, this was more travesty than transformation of the legend. Set in the 1190s but in 'an era of chivalry and of magic' that few historians of the period would recognise, *The New Adventures* mixes the Robin Hood stories, fire-breathing dragons, echoes of Arthurian mythology, kung fu fighting, miserably unfunny wisecracking and very bad special effects into one truly dreadful brew. It may have had guest stars of the calibre of Christopher Lee, who appeared in a number of episodes as a white-bearded forest sage, but nothing could disguise the fact that this was a real stinker, a cynically manufactured confection that had little to do with Robin Hood and a good deal more to do with a (failed) desire to match the kitsch charm and ratings success of what were then popular shows like *Xena: Warrior Princess*.

By the middle of the first decade of the twenty-first century, there was a need for a series that would reinterpret the legend for a new generation of TV viewers in the same way that *Robin of Sherwood* had done twenty years earlier. In 2006, the BBC broadcast the first in what were to be 39 episodes of *Robin Hood*, starring Jonas Armstrong in the title role, Lucy Griffiths as Marian, Keith Allen as the Sheriff and Richard Armitage as Sir Guy of Gisborne. The series was transmitted in the Saturday evening slot just vacated by the revived *Doctor Who* and it aimed for the same mixture of adventure and wit that had made the SF stories so successful. The main creative force behind this incarnation of Robin was Dominic Minghella, brother of the film director and playwright Anthony Minghella, and previously known primarily as the co-creator of *Doc Martin*. This was not to be a Robin Hood that would be hamstrung by tradition or a reverential attitude to previous versions of the story. The very titles of some of the episodes ('Who Shot the Sheriff?', 'Peace? Off!', 'Dead Man Walking') are enough to indicate that this is meant to be a knowingly cheeky, even flippant re-interpretation of the legend.

Another title, 'Lardner's Ring', given to an episode from the second series, pays a sneaking tribute to Ring Lardner Jr, the blacklisted American writer who provided many of the scripts for the 1950s series. Wisely, the writers (Minghella and others) make no attempt at all at authentic medieval language. It would have been necessarily unsuccessful and could only have sounded woefully stilted. Instead, the characters speak often enough in the idiom of the twenty-first century. 'In your dreams,' Marian tells Robin when he is prematurely planning her inclusion in his gang of outlaws. 'I'll show you my purse if you show me yours,' Robin says teasingly to an attractive visitor to Sherwood who turns out to be the Sheriff's sister. And meanwhile Keith Allen, as the Sheriff himself, seems set on making Alan Rickman's performance in *Robin Hood: Prince of Thieves* look subtle and restrained in comparison. He's certainly given the lines to play the pantomime villain. 'Come on, chop, chop', he admonishes an executioner who is being slow in doing his job.

Yet, beneath all the fun and the jokes and the self-conscious anachronisms, Minghella's *Robin Hood* is, in a paradoxical way, the most serious of all the TV versions of the stories. Echoes of contemporary society can be heard in every episode; parallels with the modern world abound. Its writers and creators cleverly use Robin Hood not only as a vehicle for exciting tales of adventure but as a means of exploring ideas about tolerance, justice, the relations between the sexes, the interaction between Islam and the Western world, and the gap between rich and poor that are relevant to today's reality. They do so to greater effect than many more overtly 'serious' dramas on the BBC. The series can certainly be irritating. The flipness and the writers' relentless pursuit of knowing quips can become tedious. The characterisation is sometimes so skewed towards contemporary notions of social and political correctness that it risks appearing ludicrous. Robin and his followers are all new men and women, much given to introspective examination of their emotions and to expressing their love for one another. There are times when they seem, not so much a gang of outlaws in pursuit of loot to pass on to the poor, more attendees at a psychotherapy meeting in search of the next group hug. In one particular episode, 'A Good Time to Die', the band, trapped in a barn by the Sheriff's mercenaries and facing near-certain death, engage in a truth-telling session that's closer to *One Flew Over the Cuckoo's Nest* than any traditional depiction of Robin Hood. Despite all this, the BBC series was undoubtedly a major success. It combined the kind of fast-moving family entertainment required for Saturday evening viewing with genuinely innovative re-workings of the familiar tales. It swiftly gathered a fanbase and it seems likely that its appeal will prove as long-lasting as that of *Robin of Sherwood*.

Spoofs, Parodies and Pastiches

The easiest stories to parody are those which everybody knows. If the characters in a narrative are familiar, then they can be readily subverted. Because the Robin Hood story and the characters in it are so immediately recognisable, they have long been open to pastiche and affectionate satire. They can be revisited in all sorts of guises. The outlaws can be shown as children, as they are in *Robin Hood Junior*, a Children's Film Foundation production of 1975, starring a teenage Keith Chegwin in the title role. They can be transformed into Chicago gangsters. *Robin and the Seven Hoods* from 1964 is the Rat Pack as Merry Men, an amiable updating of the story to the Prohibition era in which Frank Sinatra is Robbo, the good-hearted gangster, and Dean Martin and Sammy Davis Jr are his sidekicks John and Will. Peter Falk has fun as the villainous Guy Gisborne; Bing Crosby croons his way through several numbers as Alan A. Dale. They can be shoehorned into an SF series. In 'Qpid', an episode of *Star Trek* –

The Next Generation, Captain Picard and his crew are despatched by regular adversary Q to a simulacrum of twelfth-century England where, as Robin Hood and the Merry Men, they are forced to participate in a life-and-death game involving the rescue of Maid Marian (played by one of Picard's old flames) from the clutches of Sir Guy of Gisborne. They can even be made into the central characters in an erotic movie. *Virgins of Sherwood Forest* is a spectacularly dreadful, straight-to-video travesty of 2000, in which a female movie director is knocked unconscious and transported back to medieval times to enjoy a number of close encounters with merry men and others. (An earlier and very marginally better exercise in Sherwood soft-core is *The Ribald Tales of Robin Hood* from 1969 in which alleged actresses with names like Heidi and Bambi frolic in the forest with the outlaws.)

The stories have, of course, proved a gift to TV sketch shows. From Morecambe and Wise, as Robin and Little Ern, and Benny Hill, unhilariously poking his arrows where he shouldn't, to *Dead Ringers* mocking the anachronisms of the 2006 BBC series with scenes of Robin and the Sheriff breakdancing, the opportunities they offer to comedians have been regularly seized. In 1979, the Muppets devoted an entire show to Robin Hood. The twenty-third episode of the third series saw guest star Lynn Redgrave playing Maid Marian to Kermit's Robin as a spurned Miss Piggy, offered only the hastily concocted role of 'Sister' Tuck, fumes and schemes in the background. Fozzie Bear plays Little John and Gonzo the Sheriff of Nottingham, accidentally inflicting torture on himself rather than the captured Marian. At the end of the show, Statler, one of the two elderly hecklers always in the Muppets audience, remarks, 'The legend of Robin Hood will never die.' 'No,' replies his friend Waldorf, 'but it sure got wounded pretty bad tonight.' The exchange more or less sums up the episode. (The Muppets have returned to the stories in print. There is both a 1980 Muppet storybook and a recent sequence of Muppet comic books in which Kermit is again shown as the outlaw leader and Miss Piggy, unhampered by Lynn Redgrave, can become a porcine Maid Marian.)

In movies, we have had Hugh Paddick as Robin in *Up the Chastity Belt*, a 1971 British film starring Frankie Howerd, set 'in the lusty days of yore'. Paddick, best known as one half of the duo Julian and Sandy in the radio series *Round the Horne*, plays a limp-wristed outlaw leader in charge of a band of men significantly more gay than merry. 'Well, ducky, what do you think of our camp?' he asks Howerd, playing the medieval serf Lurkalot, when they arrive in Sherwood and 'camp' is very definitely the operative word. John Cleese appears as Robin in *Time Bandits*, the 1981 Terry Gilliam film, sounding remarkably like Prince Charles as he engages in amiable chit-chat with the midget anti-heroes of the title. 'And you're a robber too, are you?,' he inquires politely. 'How long have you been a robber?' Meanwhile, his Merry Men redistribute the spoils the Time Bandits have accumulated by handing it over to the poor. 'The poor are going to be absolutely thrilled,' he assures the central characters as they miserably watch their riches disappear.

Reversal of roles was at the heart of the BBC TV children's series *Maid Marian and Her Merry Men*, originally shown between 1989 and 1994, in which the outlaw hero has become a handsome but cowardly and fashion-obsessed tailor, Robin of Kensington. The true driving spirit behind the fight against Prince John and the Sheriff of Nottingham is Maid Marian, played by Kate Lonergan. Merry Men include a pugnacious dwarf named Little Ron, a laidback Rastafarian and a large slob called Rabies. Written by Tony Robinson, Baldric in *Blackadder*, who also throws himself into the role of the Sheriff with great relish, the series was an energetic, pantomime version of the stories. In its own, unpretentious way, it was also part of the developing trend in the 1980s and 1990s to give Maid Marian a more important role in them.

In addition to TV sketches and cameo performances in other comedy films, there are also two full length feature films which are based entirely on the idea of subverting earlier versions of the story. *The Zany Adventures of Robin Hood* starring George Segal dates from 1984. Any film that advertises itself in its title as 'zany' should probably be viewed with suspicion but this made-for-TV movie does have its moments. Peasants about to be rescued from Norman villainy regularly mistake the identity of their saviour. ('I'm not Ivanhoe,' Robin shouts at one point, 'Ivanhoe dresses in black.'); the merry men leap on their enemies with cries of 'Geronimo'; Will Scarlet, here a minstrel but an appallingly untalented one, is thwarted every time he tries to break into song. English character actors, including Roy Kinnear, Robert Hardy and Tom Baker as the villainous Sir Guy of Gisbourne, throw themselves into the spirit of the film without ever raising it above the level of mildly amusing slapstick.

The opening for a definitive Robin Hood parody was still there and, nine years later, Mel Brooks released *Robin Hood: Men in Tights*. Brooks's interest in the comic potential of the outlaw's story had been revealed in the 1970s in an ill-fated American TV series he created called *When Things Were Rotten*. Filled with the kind of sight gags and knowing anachronisms that he had already then employed in successful feature films like *Blazing Saddles*, the show failed to find much of a TV audience and was cancelled by ABC after only 13 weeks. In 1993, the recent release of the Kevin Costner version of the legend provided the ideal opportunity for Brooks to return to the subject. His penchant for poking fun at movie genres has produced some wonderful films (*Blazing Saddles, Young Frankenstein*) and some films (*Dracula: Dead and Loving It*) that are frankly poor. *Robin Hood: Men in Tights* falls somewhere between the two extremes. It's not brilliant and there are some jokes and sequences that fall woefully flat but it has enough good material in it to keep audiences laughing. Cary Elwes plays a poshly spoken Robin ('unlike some other Robin Hoods, I can speak with an English accent,' he remarks in a pointed reference to Costner's all too American tones in *Robin Hood: Prince of Thieves*) who returns from the Crusades to find his lands at the mercy of Mervyn, the wicked Sheriff of Rottingham, played by Roger Rees. Taking to the woods, he finds the Merry Men ('We're men/We're men in tights/We roam around the forest looking for fights') and becomes their leader in the struggle against the oppressive regime of the Sheriff and Prince John, neatly played by the New York stand-up Richard Lewis. Another stand-up, black comedian Dave Chappelle, plays Ahchoo, Robin's Saracen sidekick; Matthew Porretta, later to play Robin himself in the dreadful 1990s TV series *The New Adventures of Robin Hood*, is Will Scarlet O'Hara ('We're from Georgia'); Tracey Ullman is a mad crone named Latrine; and Patrick Stewart, with a Scottish accent, puts in a cameo appearance as Richard the Lionheart at the end that parallels Sean Connery's uncredited role as the king at the end of the Costner movie.

Cartoons

The very first American cartoon with a Robin Hood theme appeared the year after the Errol Flynn film in 1939. *Robin Hood Makes Good*, one of the 'Merrie Melodies' produced by Warner Brothers, is a wincingly twee tale of three young squirrels who play Robin Hood games until two of them are caught by a fox masquerading as Maid Marian. The third, and cutest, of the junior squirrels is left to rescue his brothers in an act of Hood-like heroism. This was followed by other cartoons that appropriated material from the stories. *Rabbit Hood* (1949), featuring Bugs Bunny, nods only perfunctorily in the direction of the legend and is really no more than yet another variant on the familiar storyline of the bumptious Bugs getting the better of a dim-witted opponent, in this case one who happens to be called the Sheriff of Nottingham. At the very end, the briefest of shots from the 1938 Errol Flynn film is inserted into the animation to bring matters to a conclusion. By contrast, *Robin Hood Daffy*, a Warner Brothers cartoon made nine years later, assumes a greater knowledge of the stories and even echoes a motif that dates back to the old ballads in its opening confrontation between Robin, in the shape of Daffy Duck, and Friar Tuck/Porky Pig. Most of the rest of the action follows the increasingly desperate attempts of Robin/Daffy to prove to the friar that he is who he claims to be by robbing a rich man. All his efforts rebound on him and he decides finally that life as 'Friar Duck' will be better than that of an outlaw.

Other classic cartoon characters have been given the chance to appear in Robin Hood stories over the years. In *Robin Hoodwinked* (1958), the outlaw is imprisoned in the Sheriff of Nottingham's castle, guarded only by Tom the cat. The mouse Jerry and his diaper-clad nephew Nibbles attempt to get the key from the cat and release the outlaw. Tom swallows the key and Jerry is obliged to lower Nibbles into the cat's interior to get it. Tom downs a large draught of ale and Nibbles emerges from his mouth in an intoxicated state. The mice now have the key, however, and Robin Hood, only ever seen in silhouette, escapes. Unfortunately, the cat and mouse games of Tom and Jerry never seemed so funny in an historical setting and this example is no exception to the rule. Plus Nibbles speaks with a supposed cockney accent that is very nearly as inauthentic and as irritating as Dick Van Dyke's in *Mary Poppins*. On TV the following year, Yogi Bear became *Robin Hood Yogi*, aiming to rob the rich tourists of Jellystone Park and give to the poor, 'namely ourselves', as he tells his sidekick Boo-Boo. Indeed, there was a period in the late fifties and early sixties when Hanna-Barbera, the creators of Yogi Bear and other familiar characters, seemed almost obsessed with the Robin Hood story. Drawling Huckleberry Hound was Robin Huck in a 1959 cartoon named 'Nottingham and Yeggs'; Loopy de Loop, a wolf with an extravagant French accent, enters Sherwood in search of Robin in 'Not in Nottingham' from 1962 and finds him in the shape of a squat bowman with an even more extravagant New York accent.

The Robin Hood story was flexible enough to accommodate all kinds of adaptations and transformations. In the late 1960s the Canadian company Krantz Films Inc. produced *Rocket Robin Hood*, a series of children's cartoons in which the outlaw and his band are operating in the future. In the thirtieth century, Robin is a square-jawed spaceman battling against Prince John, would-be ruler of the universe, and his henchman the Sheriff of NOTT (National Outer-space Terrestrial Territories). One intriguing contributor to the series (as uncredited writer and director) was Ralph Bakshi, the American animator who was soon to surprise fans of traditional cartoons with the X-rated *Fritz the Cat*. *Young Robin Hood*, in which the usual band of outlaws were all portrayed as teenagers, was a bland and uninspired TV cartoon made by Hanna-Barbera which ran for two series in the early nineties. At about the same time, Japanese animators turned their attention to the stories and produced *Robin Hood No Daiboken* ('Robin Hood's Great Adventure'), an anime in 52 episodes. Here too the heroes of Sherwood were largely teens and pre-teens, the kind of unnaturally wide-eyed moppets who populate so many anime. For anyone unfamiliar with the conventions of the genre, this Japanese cartoon version of the story can seem downright weird but it does include most of the characters established in the Robin Hood stories over the centuries and even some of the basic themes and motifs. The hero is Robert of Huntington, dispossessed by a wicked Nottinghamshire Norman, here identified as 'Lord Alwine'. There is a Maid Marian, a Little John and a Much. There is a Friar Tuck although, as a bear-like figure with an Irish brogue in the English translation, he looks and sounds like no other Friar Tuck ever seen on screen. Perhaps the oddest of all cartoon incarnations of Robin is one that dates from 2001. In the hugely successful, computer-animated *Shrek*, he has been transformed, for no very obvious reason, into a Frenchman, a debonair Robin des Bois complete with Gallic accent courtesy of Vincent Cassel, who attempts to rescue Princess Fiona from the eponymous ogre but discovers that she doesn't much want to be rescued.

The only full length cartoon film based on the Robin Hood stories was made by Disney in 1973. The animators created a medieval bestiary of creatures – some native to Britain, some very definitely not – to take on the roles. Robin and Marian are foxes, Little John a bear, Friar Tuck a badger, King John a lion and the Sheriff of Nottingham a wolf. At its best, Disney might have made a very good cartoon version of the stories but, by and large, the early seventies didn't see Disney at its best and this sentimental and uninventive film rarely gives the impression that those involved in it have much affection for, or knowledge of, the Robin Hood legend. By far the most irritating of its faults is the voice characterisation which was shaped by a determination to play to the US market. Robin and Marian are played by English actors and a couple of the minor characters have been equipped with grating Cockney accents but most of the leading figures speak with American voices. Alan-a-Dale, played as a rooster who is also a not particularly good country singer, is voiced by the not particularly good country singer Roger Miller. The Sheriff and Little John both have Southern drawls. Friar Tuck is played by fat cowboy actor Andy Devine and sounds as if he's just ridden in from the range. Only Peter Ustinov, as a Prince John given to tantrums and thumb-sucking, and Terry-Thomas, as his fawning snake courtier Sir Hiss, give voice performances that are both skilful and also sound right for a Robin Hood film.

Illustrated Robin

Most people have their own image of Robin Hood but there are certain elements which are common to nearly all the pictures of the iconic outlaw that individuals carry in their heads. He is a handsome, athletic figure dressed in Lincoln green or, occasionally, in red. He wears a green peaked hat, usually with a feather in it, and he carries a longbow and a quiver full of arrows on his shoulder. He is usually bearded or has a moustache. This is an image that has survived many deliberate attempts to reinvent it in recent film and TV presentations of the character and it is tempting to assume that it dates back hundreds of years. In fact, it is a relatively recent creation, an amalgam of late nineteenth-century illustrations and the images on screen in the Fairbanks and Flynn films. Throughout most of his career, nobody knew what the famous outlaw looked like nor, it seems, did they much care.

For many centuries, visual representation of Robin is either very difficult to find or so blandly generic that it lacks any real interest. It was only in the late eighteenth century that the first artist of any merit turned his attention to the outlaw and it was only in the middle decades of the following century that a tradition of depicting him was first established. Perhaps the first surviving image intended to represent Robin Hood can be found in St. Mary's Church in Beverley in the East Riding of Yorkshire. A wooden carving on a misericord which dates from c. 1450 shows two figures which scholars believe are meant to be Robin and the king standing amongst some trees. (In the other great medieval church in the town, Beverley Minster, a small stone sculpture from the previous century depicts a man with a longbow who might just conceivably be Robin but seems much more likely to be an unspecific archer.) Move forward a hundred years and a stained glass window now in the Victoria and Albert Museum, which probably dates to the middle of the sixteenth century, shows figures from the May Games. Maid Marian and Friar Tuck are clearly recognisable and some people have claimed one of the others as Robin but the identification seems, at the very least, debatable.

In the ballads, broadsides and chapbooks that proliferated over the next two centuries, Robin was often illustrated but the woodcuts that were used were common images. They were not intended to be accurate portraits of him and his associates and they were often recycled from other texts. Indeed, many of them made no gesture at all towards medievalism. In the same way that Romans on the stage in Shakespeare's day dressed like ordinary Elizabethans, Robin and his merry men were most often depicted in clothes that were contemporary with the period in which the woodcuts were printed. Ruffs, long gowns and shovel hats were in evidence rather than medieval costume. Or medieval hoods.

Visual representation of Robin began to change and become more specific in the second half of the eighteenth century. Joseph Ritson's 1795 collection of the extant ballads remains one of the most significant works on the outlaw leader ever published. Its chief importance lies, of course, in the texts that Ritson so painstakingly gathered but the illustrations to the first edition have great value in their own right. The little woodcuts which act as headpieces for some of the ballads and which are also scattered through the pages of Ritson's two volumes are by John and Thomas Bewick. Although he was one of the first men ever to earn his living almost entirely as a book illustrator, John Bewick, who died in the same year that Ritson's book was published at the age of only 35, is largely forgotten today save for his family connections. His brother Thomas, however, is still considered one of the greatest of all wood engravers, famous particularly for his images of birds and for his vignettes of the English countryside. Robin's world, as depicted by the Bewicks, continues to owe a lot to the life they saw around them. His opponent in a quarterstaff fight in the little engraving illustrating the ballad of 'Robin Hood and the Tanner', for example, looks suspiciously like a sturdy young farmer of the day. However, the Bewicks did make some attempts to situate their Robin in the past. In the same engraving the hero himself is dressed in their idea of a medieval forester's garb. On his head he has the kind of feathered hat that has since become a familiar part of the outlaw's everyday outfit. This is Robin taking his first steps on the way to becoming the immediately recognisable icon he is today.

It was the Victorian era that continued the process. Daniel Maclise's painting of 'Robin Hood Entertaining Richard the Lionheart in Sherwood Forest' was exhibited at the Royal Academy in 1839. The Irish-born Maclise was a friend of Charles Dickens and became famous for his energetic and dramatic pictures of scenes from history and literature. His Robin Hood painting was one of his first great successes. It shows Robin, the focus of the picture, toasting the king, dressed in the armour of a crusader, who sits at the foot of a tree. Other figures from the legend such as Little John and Friar Tuck are easily recognisable in the foreground. In the background a forest clearing is filled with the more anonymous members of the outlaw band. A contemporary critic, singing the painting's praises, wrote of 'how admirable are the minor details, how finely all has been imagined, how skillfully all has been executed.' In the exhibition catalogue the painting was accompanied by a quotation from a pastiche Robin Hood ballad which was printed in full in one of the magazines of the day but, looking at the painting today, the literary influence that is most apparent is Sir Walter Scott's. It was only twenty years after the publication of *Ivanhoe*. Maclise's Robin, resplendent in scarlet, may not be much like Scott's description of Locksley but the image of the merry men, surrounded by their booty and the riches of the forest as they pledge themselves to the king, carries plenty of echoes of the novel. And the whole sense of a fondly imagined medieval world of good cheer and rowdy sociability (in implicit contrast to the alienation of contemporary industrial society) owes much to Scott's fiction.

In truth, Scott's vision of the past was the major influence on historical painting for much of the nineteenth century and other Robin Hood images of the Victorian era reflect it. However, Locksley the Saxon hero was not the only way in which Robin could be portrayed. The Victorians also liked the idea of Robin as courtly lover of the greenwood, even more devoted to his Maid Marian than to his Sherwood pastimes. A prime example of this alternative nineteenth-century Robin emerged unexpectedly in 2009 when a painting by Thomas Frank Heaphy of the outlaw leader and Maid Marian was found in a broom cupboard in a Sussex working men's club. Dated to the 1860s, Heaphy's image depicts the Sherwood lovers holding hands in a forest glade. A barefooted Marian has a smile playing about her face; Robin, bearded and clad in red coat and brown leggings, gazes intently into her eyes. His hunting hounds prowl around his feet and a chest full of treasures, presumably plundered from the rich and destined for the poor, lies open on the ground. Showing the influence of the Pre-Raphaelites in his attention to painterly detail, Heaphy, a minor artist of the day, gives us a picture of Robin and Marian as the Victorians liked to imagine them.

Historical paintings, of course, reached only a relatively small audience. For Robin's iconic status to grow and develop, he had to be portrayed in other media. The period between 1880 and 1920 was a Golden Age for book illustration on both sides of the Atlantic. The success in 1883 of Howard Pyle's *The Merry Adventures of Robin Hood* in America, described earlier, was a consequence of his gifts as an artist as much as his skill as a writer. It is in Pyle's black-and-white illustrations that the outlines of the classic image of Robin Hood begin to emerge. Here is the hero in his forest attire and feathered cap. Here is the lithe and handsome athlete that later appears in the Fairbanks and Flynn films. Reproduced time and again, often with additional colouring, Pyle's illustrations embedded a particular vision of Robin in the American popular imagination. As we have seen, other illustrators in the US, many of them pupils of Pyle, produced their own versions of the outlaw in the decades that followed but they all owed at least something to the pioneering work in *The Merry Adventures of Robin Hood*. The image created at the end of the nineteenth century and the beginning of the twentieth century by Pyle, Louis Rhead, NC Wyeth and others has been a long-lasting one.

During the same period in Britain, some of the most talented and well-known illustrators of the day were also turning their attention to Robin. Arguably the most influential of all of them was Walter Crane who produced a sequence of images late on in his life for Henry Gilbert's 1912 book *Robin Hood and the Men of the Greenwood*. In many ways, Crane must have seemed the ideal artist to work on stories of an outlaw renowned for taking from the rich and giving to the poor. Early in his career, he was associated both politically and artistically with William Morris. Like Morris, he was a convinced socialist with an idealised view of the Middle Ages. In the 1890s he had published *The Claims of Decorative Art*, a polemical but successful work which attempted to show that true art could only flourish in a society where wealth was more equitably distributed. His sympathies must have been with Robin and his Merry Men but the illustrations he created for Gilbert's book are curiously subdued, even stilted, and are certainly not amongst his best work. Only the tapestry-like images of the outlaws kneeling before Richard the Lionheart and of the king joining the hands of Robin and Marian carry much conviction. The line drawings by HM Brock, a much lesser artist than Crane, which were also used to illustrate *Robin Hood and the Men of Greenwood*, actually have more vigour than the older man's work.

Crane and Brock produced their work in the last years when book and magazine illustration could be said to be as important as the cinema in shaping people's visual imaginations. Once Robin had appeared in the movies, the most popular cultural medium of the first half of the twentieth century, his image there rapidly began to dominate his image in print. However, the influence worked both ways. Robin as imagined by the illustrators of the Golden Age of Illustration affected his cinematic incarnations in the 1922 and 1938 films. The portrayals by Fairbanks and Flynn then began to feed back into the representations of Robin in books and, increasingly, comics. The first American Robin Hood comics appeared in the 1930s. The character has since made dozens of appearances in comics ranging from movie tie-ins to recreations of the legend set in post-apocalyptic futures. Superheroes and superheroines from Batman and Superman to Wonder Woman have time-travelled back to the twelfth century to meet him. One superhero, the Green Arrow, first created in 1941 and still going strong, seems to have pinched his outfit and many of his attributes from Robin Hood.

The same year that saw the debut of the Green Arrow also saw the first publication of *Classics Illustrated*, the well-known series of comic book adaptations of famous works of literature which initially appeared under the title of *Classic Comics*. The Robin Hood stories were ideal material for the new series and a *Classics Illustrated* version, based in part on Howard Pyle's perennially popular book, appeared as Issue No. 7 in December 1942. Errol

Flynn's performance as Robin was still fresh in people's minds and the original, somewhat crude illustrations obviously owed a lot to the image of the outlaw leader created by the 1938 film. The influence was even clearer when a reprint of the *Classics Illustrated* comic was published in the 1950s with new art work by Jack Sparling, an illustrator who went on to work for both of the giants of the American comic book industry, Marvel and DC. Sparling's Robin was easily recognisable as a close cousin of Flynn's. The concept of great literature in comic book form pioneered by *Classics Illustrated* has been frequently copied and very nearly every lookalike of the series that has sprung up in the last seventy years has included an issue telling the Robin Hood stories.

However, it was not just series that labelled themselves as 'Classics' that featured the outlaw. As comic books continued to become an ever more significant part of popular culture, Robin retained his place in them. In 1954, the American comic book industry, faced by a moral panic over the deleterious effects its products were supposedly having on the country's impressionable youth, brought in its own self-regulating 'Comics Code'. Since the very first provision of the code stated that, 'Crimes shall never be presented in such a way as to create sympathy for the criminal, to promote distrust of the forces of law and justice, or to inspire others with a desire to imitate criminals', it might have been thought that a charismatic outlaw, with a taste for making his opponents look very foolish indeed, would fall victim to it and be banned from the pages of the new, squeaky clean comics. In fact, the decade saw ever more Robin Hood comics on the market. Charlton Comics re-named their 'Danger and Adventure' series 'Robin Hood and His Merry Men' and ran it from 1956 to 1958. Magazine Enterprises, another second-tier publisher of comics, produced a short-lived series on Robin Hood. Although both illustrations and stories were competent enough, the series does not appear to have been a huge success. Even re-branding it by putting photographs of Richard Greene on the cover and calling it, like the TV series, 'The Adventures of Robin Hood' could not prevent it from folding in 1958 after eight issues.

The major players in the comics market turned their attention to the English outlaw too. DC Comics not only included regular stories about him in their adventure anthology comic *The Brave and the Bold* which began in 1955 and continued, in assorted incarnations, for nearly thirty years. In 1957 and 1958, they also ran a short-lived series called *Robin Hood Tales* which was entirely devoted to Sherwood's finest. Some of DC's most successful and skilful artists of the time, including Joe Kubert, Russ Heath and Ross Andru, were given the job of bringing Robin to life. They did so with considerable panache. These Robin Hood stories sometimes owed a lot more to the superhero comics genre than they did to the old ballads. There were unlikely episodes of Robin grappling with exotic beasts such as panthers and tigers and even an issue entitled 'The Masked Marvel of Sherwood Forest' in which Robin seems to have awoken one morning and decided to dress just like the Green Lantern. At the time, comic books were dismissed as tawdry rubbish but at least one Robin Hood scholar, the Canadian Allen Wright, has drawn intriguing parallels between them and the broadside ballads of earlier centuries. Like the broadsides and chapbooks of the seventeenth century, they were assumed to be crude and inartistic but they provided one of the main vehicles in the 1950s for Robin Hood to reach a new generation.

In Britain, the 1950s saw the publication of a whole host of Robin Hood comics. From the very beginning of the decade Robin was a popular subject for comic creators and the success of the Richard Greene TV series, which first aired in the autumn of 1955, only increased the character's presence on newsagents' shelves. *The Thriller Picture Library* (also known as *Thriller Comics* and

Thriller Comics Library) appeared between 1951 and 1963, beginning its life as something of a variant on the *Classics Illustrated* format and going on to embrace all kinds of adventure stories. Robin Hood was the subject of Issue Number 4 and became one of the most regularly recurring heroes in the series. Titles such as *King of Sherwood*, *Greenwood Outlaw* and *Robin Hood the Magnificent* followed. Only the Three Musketeers could match Robin in the number of issues devoted to their adventures in the twelve years the comic existed. Like most British comics of the time, *The Thriller Picture Library* had colour covers but the pages inside were all in black-and-white.

Perhaps the most striking of all these British versions were Frank Bellamy's comic strips from *Swift*, published in two series between May 1956 and August 1957. *Swift* was part of the stable of children's comics associated with *Eagle*, whose most famous character was Dan Dare, and Bellamy was an experienced and accomplished artist who had already produced re-tellings of 'The Swiss Family Robinson' and 'King Arthur and His Knights' for the comic. (He was later to graduate to *Eagle* and to illustrate Dan Dare.) Working with writer Clifford Makins, he created a version of the Robin Hood stories memorable enough to warrant republication in collected form more than fifty years later. Using as his starting point a 1940s children's novel by Charles Gilson, which combined motifs and ideas from the ballads with the author's own inventions (a villainous Norman warlord called Robert the Wolf, for example), Makins wrote the simple, readable text which accompanied Bellamy's crisp and clear, black-and-white images. The artist's Robin, striding heroically through the greenwood, still shows the influence of Errol Flynn's performance as the outlaw. Richard Todd and Richard Greene had provided artists with newer, clean-shaven models for Sherwood's hero but Robin in these two comic strips, with his pencil moustache and goatee beard, clearly harks back to the earlier film.

Meanwhile, throughout the decades when Robin was becoming a hero of the comics and beyond, he was also being regularly portrayed by illustrators of children's books. Some chose to depict Robin in the same lush colour and detail as the movies. Others took a different path and tried to pare down their work to the essentials. Arthur Hall, for instance, in his line drawings for Roger Lancelyn Green's *The Adventures of Robin Hood*, published in the 1950s, returned to the tradition of the Bewicks and produced a series of simple, deliberately naive images which complement the author's straightforward re-tellings of the tales. In 1979, Victor Ambrus, a Hungarian-born artist who was later to become known for his work on *Time Team*, the Channel 4 archaeological programme, produced illustrations for *Robin Hood: His Life and Legend* by Bernard Miles. Like Hall, he clearly wanted to get away from the Hollywood image of Robin, echoed in so many comics and book illustrations, but, instead of visual simplicity, he opted for detail. Like the reconstructions of archaeological sites he went on to create for *Time Team*, his Robin illustrations are exercises in finely-drawn, gritty realism. Ambrus's Merry Men look as if they might indeed be medieval outlaws, their clothes plastered with the dirt of the forest, rather than the movie extras frolicking through photogenic parkland that other illustrators depict.

In the last thirty years, new and sometimes challenging images of Robin have continued to appear in print. Well-known illustrators such as Tony Ross, Michael Foreman and Helen Craig have produced their versions of him and he has been depicted in everything from pop-up books to historical fiction for young adults. As comic books have morphed into graphic novels, with a concurrent rise in literary and artistic respectability, he has remained a subject that has attracted creative attention. *Demons of Sherwood* (2009) started life as a webcomic but has since appeared in book form. Written by Robert Tinnell, a screenwriter and director with an interest in the horror genre, and illustrated by Bo Hampton, a comic book artist who has worked on the Batman franchise, this is a revisionist Robin Hood story in which the legendary hero, his glory days in the past, has become a drink-soaked loser. Only when Marian is threatened with burning at the stake as a witch does he pull himself together sufficiently to join forces with his comrades of old (Little John, Tuck, Scarlet, etc.) to rescue her. But saving Marian proves to be just the beginning of a series of adventures which neatly and amusingly combine old-fashioned swashbuckling with elements of horror.

Outlaw by Tony Lee, Sam Hart and Artur Fujita, also published in 2009, is a graphic novel that puts together its story of Robin's return from the crusades, to revenge his father's death and become a hero of the greenwood, from an eclectic mix of sources. Some elements are borrowed from the traditional stories, some from Hollywood films, some from the *Robin of Sherwood* TV series and some seem to be the inventions of writer Tony Lee. The depictions of Robin himself are a little disappointing and lacking in individuality – there are even times when it is difficult to distinguish the outlaw leader from other characters – but the book does contain some vividly evocative and colourful panels of life in his world. Rich washes of green flood through the scenes set in Sherwood; darker blues and purples create menacing shadows within the walls of Nottingham Castle where the Sheriff and Sir Guy of Gisbourne plot the hero's downfall. *Outlaw* is a powerful re-telling of the legend in graphic novel format and marks another stage in the long history of the visual representation of Robin Hood.

Musical Robin

Did the Robin Hood stories begin in music? To the modern ear, the word 'ballad' suggests that the early tales of the outlaw were written to be sung but that was not necessarily the case. In the late medieval era, a ballad was not, by definition, something that had to be sung. In fact, the very earliest of the Robin Hood ballads were almost certainly intended to be recited rather than sung. However, many of them may well have been recited to a musical accompaniment. The ritual dramas of the May Games, in many of which Robin and Marian and Friar Tuck came to play significant roles, would also have been performed to the sound of drums and pipes and other early musical instruments. So music provided background to the Robin Hood legend from the very beginning and, as new ballads were created throughout the seventeenth and eighteenth centuries, new musical settings would have been made for the words. The persistence of this music through the years was remarkable. When folk music revivalists in the 1890s and early 1900s such as Ralph Vaughan Williams and Cecil Sharp began to write down songs they heard from singers in English country villages, they found settings of many Robin Hood ballads including 'Robin Hood and the Tanner', 'Robin Hood and the Bishop' and 'Robin Hood and the Pedlar'. Some of these tunes had been handed down through families for generations and may well have dated back as far as the words.

It was in the eighteenth century, however, that Robin found a new musical home outside the broadside ballads. He became a relatively familiar figure on the London stage, most frequently seen in what would probably today be called 'musicals' but were then described as 'comic operas'. In 1730, a work called *Robin Hood and Little John* was performed at Bartholomew Fair. Little is known about it but only two years had passed since the exceptional success of John Gay's ballad opera *The Beggar's Opera* and it may well have been an enterprising attempt to cash in on the consequent popularity of stage productions featuring amiable rogues and tricksters. Twenty years later and Robin had kissed farewell to the plebeian clamour of the fair and gone significantly upmarket. In 1750, he stepped onto the stage of the Drury Lane Theatre, then under the management of the legendary actor David Garrick, in a piece entitled *Robin Hood: A New Musical Entertainment*. Written by Moses Mendez, with music by Charles Burney, a minor composer, musicologist and father of the novelist Fanny Burney, this was a short work intended to be performed after the audience had enjoyed the longer play at the heart of the evening's entertainment. Carrying faint echoes of the old ballad telling the story of Robin and Alan-a-Dale, Mendez's plot featured the outlaw hero working to free the beautiful Clarinda from forced marriage to a foppish cad named Glitter and to unite her with the handsome Leander. The work concludes with everyone gathered in Sherwood Forest where true love is able to triumph. Although it was an afterpiece to the main entertainment, the musical was more than just a negligible trifle. Mendez's lyrics were witty and well written and Burney's music was skilful and demanding. At least two of the singers in the piece – the soprano Kitty Clive playing Clarinda and the tenor John Beard taking the title role – were major figures in London musical life at the time who both performed at premieres of Handel's operas and oratorios.

In the last decades of the century, new musicals involving the outlaw hero continued to appear. Charles Dibdin's *Robin Hood*, performed at the impressively-named Royal Circus and Equestrian

Philharmonic Academy on Blackfriars Road in 1783, may well have boasted onstage horses to increase the spectacle it provided. By far the most successful of these eighteenth century musicals featuring Robin, however, was Leonard Macnally and William Shield's *Robin Hood, or, Sherwood Forest* which opened at Covent Garden in April 1784. Long runs were not the norm at the time but this comic opera was regularly staged in London over a period of sixteen years. Touring companies took it around the UK and across the seas to Ireland and the USA. Even as late as 1820, audiences in Bath were enjoying a revival of it. Macnally claimed that he took his plot from old ballads. He would certainly have had the chance to consult some collections of them that appeared in the 1770s but his Robin, once again the exiled Earl of Huntington, owes more to the gentrified tradition that had developed since Munday's plays than he does to the yeoman outlaw of the ballads. Maid Marian never appears in the opera and is given only an undignified mention as a servant making pastry for a feast. Robin's lover is Clorinda, arriving on stage dressed as an archer and teasingly informing Little John that, 'I come to seek with bended bow/That man of might/I fain would fight/And conquer with my oh ho ho!' Other female characters absent from traditional versions of the story, although not so eager as Clorinda to proclaim the delights of their 'oh ho ho!', must have added to the appeal of the opera. William Shield's music, a skilful melange of his own work and borrowings from other composers and traditional melodies, also gave it a boost that made it one of the most popular stage pieces of its day. (Interestingly, Shield was a friend of Joseph Ritson, who was to produce his great collection of Robin Hood ballads ten years after the opera's premiere, and had collaborated with him in gathering together volumes of English and Scottish songs.)

It was in the late eighteenth century that the traditional English pantomime began to take shape and the presence of Robin Hood in the comic operas of the period meant that he also became available as a character for pantomime. In the nineteenth century, comic operas featuring Robin and the characters from the legend did continue to appear. Peacock's novel *Maid Marian* was given a stage version soon after publication in 1822 and this was successful enough to be translated into both French and German. However, by the Victorian era, Robin's most frequent appearances on stage were in pantomimes. Nearly all of these included songs and extensive musical interludes. By the middle of the century the comic opera, as experienced by the original audience for Macnally and Shield's *Robin Hood*, had, in effect, been overtaken by the pantomime but the outlaw was still a figure in the new form. In 1860, one of the first works by FC Burnand, later to be a grand old man of the Victorian stage and the editor of *Punch* magazine, was a Robin Hood pantomime.

Robin could also take his place in more serious works of musical theatre. In the same year that the young Burnand was producing his pantomime, a three-act opera entitled *Robin Hood*, with words by John Oxenford and music by George Macfarren, was first staged at Her Majesty's Theatre, London. Macfarren, now largely forgotten, was a successful Victorian composer of all kinds of music from light orchestral works to oratorios. He produced a dozen operas, including several such as *King Charles II* from 1849 on subjects from English history. Oxenford, a dramatist and librettist whose first works had appeared in the 1830s, had once been a theatre critic for *The Times* and was an expert on German literature and philosophy. Their opera focused on the love between Robin and Marian, although the plot was given an unusual twist by making Marian the daughter of the Sheriff of Nottingham. It also made extensive use of the conflict between Saxon and Norman that had become so central a part of the Robin Hood story in the four decades since the publication of Scott's *Ivanhoe*. 'The grasping, rasping Norman race' is condemned in one aria and Robin becomes the vehicle for Victorian patriotism and ideas about liberty-loving Englishman when he sings in Act I that, 'Englishmen by birth are free;/Though their limbs you chain,/Glowing thoughts of liberty/In their hearts remain.' Macfarren and Oxenford's *Robin Hood* proved popular enough with audiences for piano transcriptions of its best numbers to be published (Robin Hood quadrilles and Robin Hood waltzes based on Macfarren's music also appeared) but its popularity was short-lived. It never achieved any kind of place in the operatic repertoire and a recent CD of it made by Victorian Opera Northwest, a society of enthusiasts for nineteenth-century English opera, was a record of the first performance of the work in more than a century.

A far more significant English composer than Macfarren, Sir Arthur Sullivan (of Gilbert and Sullivan fame) shared the cultural interest of the period in an idealised version of the English Middle Ages and, when he was looking for a subject for his long-planned grand opera, he chose *Ivanhoe* with its supporting role for a tenor as the outlaw Locksley. Scott's novel had already provided inspiration for composers on the Continent and Rossini, Heinrich Marschner and Otto Nicolai had produced versions of it for the operatic stage. Now Sullivan, determined to create a large-scale historical work, decided to adapt it. Julian Sturgis, an American-born novelist and lyricist who also holds the unlikely distinction of having been the first American to play in an FA Cup Final (in his youth, he was an amateur footballer for The Wanderers), wrote the libretto. The opera had its premiere in January 1891, the first work to be staged in the new Royal English Opera House, now the Palace Theatre in Cambridge Circus. Accepted opinion on Sullivan's *Ivanhoe* tends to be that it was a failure and he should have stuck to the comic operas at which he was so skilled but, in fact, it ran for more than 150 consecutive performances after this premiere. Although it rapidly fell out of the repertoire, there have been attempts to revive it recently. Critics have highlighted its significance in the history of English opera and complete recordings of it have been issued in the last few years. Sullivan himself returned to Robin Hood in 1893 when he wrote incidental music for the Tennyson play *The Foresters*.

However, it was not just in England that the outlaw provided a subject for opera in the second half of the nineteenth century. Albert Dietrich was a German composer, born in 1829, who studied with Robert Schumann and was a close friend of Brahms. His three-act *Robin Hood* was first staged in Frankfurt in 1879. Rarely performed since this premiere, it was revived in Erfurt in 2011. More significantly the prolific American composer Reginald De Koven produced a comic opera entitled *Robin Hood* in Chicago in 1890. De Koven had studied in England as a young man and was an admirer of Gilbert and Sullivan so it is perhaps no great surprise that his musical take on the legend was a success when it was staged in London at the Prince of Wales Theatre the following year. The opera remained popular with audiences for years to come and was staged in very nearly every major US city in the 1890s and 1900s. (At least one song from it, 'Oh Promise Me' which Robin sings to Marian, was regularly performed at weddings for decades after that and was recorded in the 1940s and 1950s by artistes as different as Nelson Eddy and The Platters.) Together with Howard Pyle's immensely successful re-telling of the stories in *The Merry Adventures of Robin Hood*, De Koven's light opera was instrumental in the process of transforming the outlaw into a hero that appealed to Americans as much as to the English, a process consolidated in 1922 by Douglas Fairbanks's cinematic triumph as Robin.

The twentieth and twenty-first centuries have seen Robin inspire work by all kinds of musicians. Classical composers such as Michael Tippett have chosen to use him in their music. Tippett was born in 1905 and his first opera emerged from his work in

Yorkshire mining communities ravaged by unemployment during the 1930s. After helping a group to stage a version of John Gay's *The Beggar's Opera*, he went on to write his own ballad opera of *Robin Hood*, first performed by villagers, miners and students in Boosbeck, North Yorkshire in 1934. In Tippett's words at the time, the work 'enabled me to reinterpret the legend of the famous outlaw in terms of the class war then dividing English society' but the composer later came to see it as an apprentice piece and refused to let it be performed. Robin was an ideal hero for the 1930s but, for decades, there was no other opera which featured him. However, in the last ten years, the gap has been filled, perhaps surprisingly, by two European composers of modern classical music. In 2007, the Komische Oper in Berlin staged a children's opera in fifteen scenes by Frank Schwemmer in which a young boy, playing a computer game about the hero, presses a wrong key and is plunged back into medieval Sherwood Forest where he joins forces with Robin to defeat Prince John. Four years later, the Finnish composer and big band leader Jukka Linkola produced a comic opera *Robin Hood* at the Finnish National Opera House in Helsinki which made use of the traditional stories but also added new characters such as a Saracen girl who assists the hero and, a more unlikely addition to the cast list, the Sheriff of Nottingham's mother.

During the decades when he was absent from the operatic stage, Robin continued to be a popular subject for pantomimes and there was also at least one attempt to construct a musical around the character. In the 1960s, searching for a follow-up to his spectacular success with *Oliver!*, the songwriter and composer Lionel Bart chose to write about Robin Hood, depicting the folk hero as a medieval con-man. Unfortunately, he gave it the title *Twang!*. Worse even than his choice of title was Bart's decision to use his own money to finance the musical and to sign away the rights to *Oliver!* to ensure that the new show was put on. The omens for the musical were not good. 'Do you know what it's like bringing this show into London?', one producer said. 'It's like giving a crazy man £30,000 and having him flush the notes down the toilet one by one.' The sceptical producer was right. Opening in 1965, *Twang!* was mercilessly rubbished by the critics and was a disastrous flop. However, the passing years have shown that Bart may just have been ahead of his time. Other musical versions of the legend have followed. West End impresario Bill Kenwright commissioned *Robin: Prince of Sherwood* from Rick Fenn and Peter Howarth in the 1990s and it went on to have a respectable run at the Piccadilly Theatre. The introduction of a witch named Morgana and a chorus of 'Satanists' and 'Sisters of Sodom' may have had something to do with its appeal. In the last ten years, *Robin Hood – Das Musical* has also been one of the success stories of the German musical theatre.

Throughout the twentieth century, of course, Robin has achieved his biggest impact not on stage but on the screen. The music which has accompanied his cinematic and TV exploits over the years has undoubtedly played its part in creating the outlaw's status in the popular imagination. By most rational criteria, the theme song for the 1950s TV series starring Richard Greene is dreadful. The lyrics ('Robin Hood, Robin Hood/Riding through the glen/Robin Hood, Robin Hood/With his band of men') are silly doggerel. What's Robin doing riding through a (Scottish) glen other than providing an easy rhyme for 'men' in the later line? The cheerily but daftly catchy tune, composed by the American songwriter Carl Sigman, seems fit only for the parody that the Monty Python people made of it. ('Dennis Moore, Dennis Moore/Galloping through the sward/Dennis Moore, Dennis Moore/And his horse Concorde'.) And yet not only did the song provide a top 20 hit for Dick James in the 1950s, it has since become arguably the best-known piece of music ever associated with the outlaw. Its chief rival for the accolade – 'Everything I Do

I Do It For You', the wildly inappropriate but hugely successful ballad sung by Bryan Adams at the end of *Robin Hood: Prince of Thieves* – is equally awful, although the rest of Michael Kamen's music for that film is often very good.

Other talented film composers, including John Barry (*Robin and Marian*) and Clifton Parker (*The Story of Robin Hood and His Merrie Men*), have worked on Robin movies and Andy Price's heroically energetic music is one of the great successes of the recent BBC TV series. However, the man who was undoubtedly the finest composer to produce music to accompany Robin Hood on screen was Erich Wolfgang Korngold. Born in what is now the Czech Republic in 1897, Korngold was a child prodigy who produced his first ballet at the age of eleven and two well-received operas before he was out of his teens. His opera *Die Tote Stadt* was a huge international success in 1920. He went to Hollywood for the first time in 1934 to work on the Max Reinhardt film version of *A Midsummer Night's Dream*, adapting Mendelssohn's incidental music for the play and introducing his own to a finished score. He stayed to work on music for other films, including the Errol Flynn swashbuckler *Captain Blood* and he was the obvious choice to produce the score for *The Adventures of Robin Hood* in 1938. The richly romantic music he wrote for the film won him an Oscar. Although he returned to more traditional classical music in his later life (he wrote a Violin Concerto, a Cello Concerto and a Symphony amongst other works), Korngold was never dismissive of his scores for Hollywood. He had large ambitions for them and always believed that they could be performed successfully in the concert hall. He died in 1957, at a time when the best film music was rarely given the credit it deserved, but his confidence in his work has proved justified. Starting in the 1970s, Korngold's Hollywood music has been reassessed. Concert performances and recordings of his major scores, including that for *The Adventures of Robin Hood,* have followed.

So Robin, in the last hundred years, has provided the inspiration for musicians ranging from a *wunderkind* of the late Austro-Hungarian empire to the Cockney composer of *Oliver!*, from one of the giants of twentieth-century English classical music to a Finnish jazz pianist. It's perhaps best to conclude this chapter with a reminder of where musical Robin began. Before he was the subject of eighteenth-century ballad operas, before he took a tenor role in Sir Arthur Sullivan's attempt at grand opera, before he rode across the cinematic screen to the accompaniment of Korngold's soaring melodies, Robin was a figure in English folk music. As Cecil Sharp and Ralph Vaughan Williams discovered when they toured the villages of Somerset and Dorset and other counties, folk musicians had been singing Robin's praises for generations. The tradition has continued. The Irish band Clannad drew extensively on the English folk tradition in creating the music for the 1980s TV series *Robin of Sherwood* and their BAFTA-winning album *Legend*, gathering together this music, was a great success. Other exponents of folk rock have produced their Robin songs. Steeleye Span's 'Gamble Gold', for instance, a track from their most famous album *All Around My Hat*, is a version of the old ballad entitled 'The Bold Pedlar and Robin Hood'. Robin, the hero of English folk music, in all likelihood, will survive well into the future.

Computer Robin and the Future of a Legend

Legends only survive through the centuries if successive generations can find something meaningful and inspirational within them. They only survive when people can adapt them to new social circumstances and, perhaps even more importantly, to new technologies. For more than six hundred years, men and women have been reinventing and reshaping the Robin Hood story for changing times. When printing arrived at the end of the fifteenth century, Robin made the transition from oral ballad to printed broadside. When the stage developed as an important cultural medium in the Shakespearean era, he became a character on stage. After cinema began at the end of the nineteenth century, it was not long before Robin Hood stories were being written for the new medium. If Robin is going to survive into the future, he needs to find his place in a world where computers dominate. Signs that he will easily do so are very promising.

Board games based on Robin's adventures have been around for many decades. Any upsurge of interest in the character following a particularly successful film or TV series has always been accompanied by an increase in the production of Robin Hood merchandise. Games have appeared in the 1930s on the back of the Errol Flynn film, in the 1950s as a consequence of the popularity of the Richard Greene TV series and in the 1970s because of the Disney animated feature. It was important for their future that, with the advent of video and computer games, Robin and his Merry Men should be used as characters in these new formats. They soon put in their appearance. The first video game to feature them was produced in the early 1980s. More than a dozen have followed. Some, like their dice and board predecessors, have been based on Robin stories in other media. A 1985 game for the Amstrad took its inspiration from the *Robin of Sherwood* TV series. A Virgin game from 1991 for the Nintendo Entertainment System was called *Robin Hood: Prince of Thieves* and was an authorised offshoot from the Kevin Costner movie of the same title.

However, the most important games as an indication of Robin's future are those which are not directly linked to his appearances in cinema or on the TV but which show the character being used only in a new medium. The last decade has seen the release of more than a dozen such Robin games. Not all have been successful. *Robin Hood: Defender of the Crown*, created by Cinemaware in 2003, was a remade version of an earlier medieval game, simply called *Defender of the Crown*, which had been a big moneyspinner for the company in the late 1980s. Second time around, game critics were not hugely impressed. They were even less enamoured of *Robin Hood's Quest*, an adventure game for PlayStation which came out in 2007. One writer on a games website described it uncompromisingly as an 'almost entirely unplayable piece of garbage'. Luckily for Robin fans who are also games enthusiasts, there have been successful releases. *Robin Hood: The Legend of Sherwood* from 2002, for instance, is an award-winning strategy game devised by the German games developer Spellbound. Based on a premise familiar from dozens of print and cinema versions of the stories (that Robin is a crusader returned to England who finds his inheritance has been seized by the chief villain), the game allows players to control characters like Robin himself, Maid Marian, Friar Tuck, Little John and others as they attempt to outwit the Sheriff of Nottingham and Prince John. And, as the platforms for games increase in number and variety, so each one seems to get its Robin Hood game. *Robin Hood: The Return of Richard* is a shooting game for Wii and the iPhone, although again the reviews of it were not particularly kind.

In a sense, the fact that Robin has been featured both in games that have been utterly slated by the critics and in games that have met with considerable approval is a sign that the character has successfully made the transition to a new medium. The history of Robin at the cinema is more than just the tale of big productions like the Flynn film and the Ridley Scott version; it also includes cheap Hammer movies and low-budget sixties swashbucklers from Italy. The more Robin computer games there are, the merrier. Meanwhile *Sherwood Dungeon*, a free-to-play MMORPG (Massively Multi-player Online Role-Playing Game), set in a medieval fantasy world, borrows its name, if very little else, from the old stories, and is produced by a company calling itself Maid Marian Entertainment. Robin has very definitely migrated into the digital and online world and, in years to come, the stories will adapt themselves to the new media as they did when the movies first arrived. The signs of a lasting legend are its flexibility and openness to change and the tales of Robin Hood have long shown that they possess these qualities in abundance.

Merry Men (and Others)

Little John

The figure of Little John, Robin's huge and trusted lieutenant, makes his appearance in the earliest of the ballads and stories. He is present in the Gest, where he is one of the men who initially capture the knight Sir Richard of the Lee. Indeed, he is the focus of one section of the poem when the narrative attention turns away from Robin and follows Little John as he wins an archery contest, takes service with the Sheriff, and eventually lures the outlaws' most famous opponent into Sherwood. John is also the only one of Robin's band to be mentioned in the earliest references to the outlaw in historical chronicles. His presence there and his importance in the Gest, where he is the hero of a quite distinct episode, both suggest that there may once have been a separate tradition of stories about him in which his name was not necessarily linked with that of Robin. If there was, it has been lost.

The most famous story about John, which explains both his name and the origins of his friendship with Robin, dates to a later period than the *Gest*. It is first found in a ballad which probably dates to the middle of the seventeenth century, although there may well have been earlier versions of it which didn't survive. In 'Robin Hood and Little John', the outlaw leader encounters a giant, seven feet tall, on a narrow bridge over a brook. Neither man is prepared to give way and they fight with quarter staffs. The giant knocks Robin off his feet and into the stream but both adversaries are so delighted with the rough-and-tumble bout that they become fast friends. The tall man reveals that his name is John Little but one of Robin's band, Will Stutely, jokes that he should rather be called Little John and the name sticks. The brawl on the bridge has become one of the most popular of all scenes from the Robin Hood legend and is repeated again and again in books and on screen. It is a rare version of the story that does not include it.

Like his master, Little John has had his name given to a number of features of the landscape of northern England (Little John's Cave, Little John's Well, etc.) but the place that has been most often associated with him is Hathersage, a village in the Derbyshire Peak District. He is reputedly buried in the churchyard there. Although this is unlikely to be 'true', the tradition that it is has been around for a long time. The story is mentioned as early as 1620 and, later in the century, the antiquarian Elias Ashmole, founder of the Ashmolean Museum in Oxford, wrote that, 'Little John lyes buried in Hathersage Churchyard within three miles from Castleton, near High Peake, with one stone set up at his head and another at his feete, but a large distance between them.'

John has been a near-indispensable figure in the legend for close to six centuries. Very nearly all plays, poems and novels about the Sherwood outlaws include him. (Although, curiously, Walter Scott ignores him almost completely in *Ivanhoe*. There is only the briefest throwaway reference to the fact that he is away on the borders of Scotland when the events of the novel take place.) When Robin Hood became a movie hero, his second-in-command was once again at his side. The best-known Little John on screen was Alan Hale, the American character actor who took the role in Douglas Fairbanks's silent movie of 1922 and was still playing it nearly thirty years later. Hale, who first stepped before a camera in 1911 and went on to appear in more than 230 films in his career, was also a rumbustious Little John to Errol Flynn's

Robin in 1938. Fittingly, his last screen appearance was as the character he had made his own. In 1950, the year he died, Hale played Little John once more in *Rogues of Sherwood Forest*. Little John has been increasingly sidelined in screen versions of the last fifty years. In the 1950s TV version, Archie Duncan's John is still quite clearly right hand man to Richard Greene's Robin and Clive Mantle has a significant part to play in *Robin of Sherwood* in the 1980s. However, in the Kevin Costner film in 1991, his place as most loyal lieutenant has been rather usurped by the Saracen Azeem. And in the 2006 BBC series, Little John, as played by Gordon Kennedy, is often not much more than a big man who stands in the background when Robin is delivering rousing speeches to the Merry Men. Other characters attract more of the limelight.

Friar Tuck

Friar Tuck does not appear in the Gest nor does he appear in any of the very early ballads. The character was certainly known in the early fifteenth century. The royal writs of 1417 refer to a chaplain from Sussex named Robert Stafford who adopted the alias of 'Frere Tuk' when he was the leader of an outlaw band in the county. However, the friar seems to have become associated with Robin Hood through the May Games rather than through the ballad tradition. The first clear record of Tuck as one of the Merry Men is in the fragmentary playscript usually entitled 'Robyn Hod and the Shryff of Nottingham'. This is thought to date from about 1475 and to be a partial record of one of the folk dramas about Robin and his men that were regularly performed in the fifteenth and sixteenth centuries. Because of the fragmentary nature of the piece, it is difficult to interpret but Tuck's role appears to be to attack the Sheriff and his men with his bow. 'Behold wele Frere Tuke', one outlaw says, 'Howe he doth his bowe pluke.' In these plays, action mattered much more than words and we can imagine the person playing the ecclesiastic engaging in vigorous mime as these words were being spoken.

The first record of Tuck in a ballad has to wait until the seventeenth century, although 'Robin Hood and the Curtal Friar' may well have existed in earlier versions that have not survived. In it, Robin forces a friar at Fountains Abbey to carry him on his back across a stream. When they are halfway across, the friar hurls his passenger into the water and the two launch themselves on a fight which only ends when Robin, impressed by his foe's valour, invites him to join the Merry Men. In the ballad, the friar is never named as Tuck but the story has nonetheless become the most familiar of all those involving the fat cleric and it makes an appearance in many of the books and films perpetuating the legend in the last century and a half. (It probably owes much of its popularity to Howard Pyle's use of it in *The Merry Adventures of Robin Hood*.)

In the nineteenth century, Friar Tuck became firmly established as a crucial character in the stories. He appears in *Ivanhoe* under the guise of the ebullient Clerk of Copmanhurst and in Peacock's novel *Maid Marian* as the title character's spiritual adviser. Ironically, as the Robin Hood stories, in the course of the century, became more and more firmly associated with the reign of Richard the Lionheart, Tuck became, in effect, an almost ever-present anachronism. He nearly always had a role to play but, since mendicant friars did not appear in England until well after Richard I's reign, he shouldn't really have been around to take it. However, few people seem to have been bothered by the historical inaccuracy and, when the movie versions of Robin's story began to appear, Tuck proved once again an essential element. In nearly all the adaptations of the Robin Hood story that have appeared on screen, he has been portrayed as a fat, ale-loving *bon vivant* and the actors who have taken the role, from Eugene Pallette in the 1938 film to Mike McShane in *Robin Hood:*

Prince of Thieves, have all tended to be almost as notable for their girth as for their thespian talents. The one significant exception to the rule that Friar Tuck should be played as plump and jolly is the casting of black actor David Harewood as a version of the character in the third season of the recent BBC TV series.

Maid Marian

Everyone knows that Robin Hood has his Maid Marian but the close association between the two of them is actually more recent than many people suspect. Like Friar Tuck, Marian is conspicuous by her absence from the Gest and the early ballads and it seems almost certain that she was first paired with Robin in the May Games. In turn, scholars have traced her character in these folk dramas back to an old French tradition of a shepherdess called Marion who had her own Robin, a shepherd rather than an outlaw. *Le Jeu de Robin et Marion* by a poet named Adam de la Halle, for example, dates from the late thirteenth century. Somehow, knowledge of the character and her link with another character named Robin made the journey across the Channel and was incorporated into the performances of the May Games.

Yet the association was not necessarily fixed. Even as late as the first decade of the sixteenth century, one Alexander Barclay could write of 'some merry fytte of Maid Marian or else of Robin Hood' which suggests that he saw them as belonging to two different narratives. Move forward another century and a half, and ballads were being printed in which Robin had a lady love, indeed a wife, but her name was not Marian. In 'Robin Hood's Birth, Breeding, Valour and Marriage', Robin engages in a rather coy but successful courtship of a feisty, buck-hunting young woman named Clorinda and the same name was used in some of the ballad operas of the eighteenth century. 'Robin Hood and Maid Marian' is the only ballad in which the outlaw's lover plays a part under her familiar name. It dates from the second half of the seventeenth century and reads as if it was written as a deliberate attempt to create a place in the ballad tradition for a character who was already known from other literary genres. Anthony Munday had included her in his play *The Downfall of Robert, Earl of Huntington* in the 1590s where he makes Robin's love 'chaste Matilda, the Lord Fitzwater's daughter', and 'afterwardes his faire Maide Marian'. It may well be significant that 'Robin Hood and Maid Marian' is one of the very few ballads which gentrify Robin. It too refers to him as the Earl of Huntington. Telling a tale in which she ventures into the greenwood dressed as a page boy and fights with a disguised Robin, it provides an early example of Maid Marian as a mettlesome and independent woman.

It was the nineteenth century that turned Marian into a rather insipid love interest, pushed to the background while Robin and the Merry Men engaged in fighting, feasting and male bonding. In some of the most influential interpretations of the old stories, she has no role at all to play. As noted previously, Howard Pyle chose to exclude her from his book *The Merry Adventures of Robin Hood* altogether, apart from the briefest of passing mentions. The relegation of Marian to decorative supporting player, or less, continued when film became the principal means of telling the story. Even in the Warner Brothers movie of 1938, Olivia de Havilland is little more than a pretty prize to reward Errol Flynn's Robin for his swashbuckling heroics. It is only in on-screen performances in the last decade, such as Lucy Griffiths' in the 2006 BBC series and Cate Blanchett's in the 2010 Ridley Scott film, and in the deliberately feminist novels of the last twenty years like Jennifer Roberson's *Lady of the Forest* and Robin McKinley's *The Outlaws of Sherwood*, that Marian regains the spirit and vitality she originally had. However, perhaps the most improbable of all incarnations of Maid Marian is also one of the most recent. Supermodel Kate Moss fetchingly donned a forester's outfit but struggled to give conviction to her handful of lines when she appeared in a cameo role as Robin's sweetheart in the 1999 time-travel comedy *Blackadder: Back and Forth*.

Will Scarlet

Will Scarlet is one of the first of the merry men, associated with Robin from the very earliest ballads. In the Gest, he assists in the capture of Sir Richard at the Lee, although the name is given there as Will Scarlock. Indeed, Will is the merry man whose name seems most flexible. He appears regularly in other ballads but under such various identities as Will Scathelocke, Will Scadlock and Will Scatheloke. This has caused nothing but confusion in later versions of the story. Anthony Munday, in his plays of the 1590s, featured both a Scarlet and a Scathlocke as half-brothers. Three hundred years later, Howard Pyle also made them two separate individuals. To add to the complications surrounding the character, Will Stutely, who is one of the merry men in several ballads, and appears both in Pyle's book and in plenty of other re-tellings, may well be no more than yet another corrupted variant of Will Scarlet's name.

The ballad 'Robin Hood and Will Scarlet' provides a story to explain Will's arrival in Sherwood. Robin is walking in the forest when he meets 'a deft young man' whose 'stockings like scarlet shone'. The young man is hunting deer with his bow and, when he downs a buck with a particularly good shot, Robin offers him a place among the merry men. The young man turns down the opportunity and the two men fight. Robin is getting the worst of it when he asks his opponent about himself. The stranger replies that his name is Young Gamwell and that he has come to the woods to seek out his uncle whom some call Robin Hood. Robin owns up to being that very man and the two of them throw down their arms and embrace. When Little John arrives on the scene, eager as ever for a scrap, Robin acknowledges Young Gamwell as 'my own dear sister's son'. He tells John that the newcomer 'shall be a bold yeoman of mine/My chief man next to thee' and that 'Scarlet he shall be', presumably because of the colour of his stockings. Although this is not one of the early ballads and its narrative is no more than a variant on a recurring one in which Robin encounters a stranger in the forest who ends up as a member of his band, the story has been used in many re-tellings over the centuries.

Most of the film and TV versions of the story find room for Will Scarlet in the cast. In the Errol Flynn movie of 1938, David Niven was originally pencilled in to play the role but he was holidaying in England at the time of filming and the job eventually went to Patric Knowles. More recently, Christian Slater in *Robin Hood: Prince of Thieves* is a Will Scarlet who turns out to be Robin's brother. (The tradition of making Will some kind of relation of Robin, established in the seventeenth-century ballad, has continued.) On TV, Paul Eddington, later famous for *The Good Life* and *Yes, Minister*, appeared as Will in the fourth series of the 1950s series. A young Ray Winstone, playing an inexplicably Cockney Will, gave what is still the most energetic and vigorous of all onscreen portrayals of the character in *Robin of Sherwood*.

The Sheriff of Nottingham

The Sheriff was established as Robin's chief antagonist in the earliest of the ballads, appearing in the Gest (in which the outlaw eventually kills him and strikes off his head) and in others such as 'Robin Hood and the Potter' and 'Robin Hood and Sir Guy of Gisborne'. Just as many historians have pursued the will-of-the-wisp figure of the 'real' Robin Hood, so various attempts have been made to identify an actual Sheriff of Nottingham, present in the historical record, who could have been the outlaw's great enemy. One of the names most frequently cited is that of Philip Mark who was Sheriff of Nottinghamshire and Derbyshire from 1209 to 1224 but other candidates (Roger de Lacy, William

Brewer, Eustace of Lowdham) have also had their advocates. In truth, the Sheriff is important only insofar as he represents the corrupt authority against which Robin and his men are fighting. His 'real' identity is almost irrelevant.

In literature, the character has occasionally lost the prominence he had in the early ballads. Some writers have ignored him altogether. However, from the late nineteenth century onwards, most children's versions of the stories have identified him as the chief villain. In the movies and on TV, the Sheriff has sometimes been ignored in favour of other bad guys (in the 1938 film, Basil Rathbone's virile Guy of Gisbourne completely overshadows Melville Cooper's wimpish and cowardly Sheriff) but he has also been played on a number of occasions with considerable style and panache. Villains are often much more satisfying to play than heroes and, over the years, the Sheriff has provided a number of actors with the ideal opportunity to enjoy themselves in the depiction of cold-hearted cynicism and nastiness. Nickolas Grace in *Robin of Sherwood* in the 1980s and Keith Allen in the recent BBC *Robin Hood* series have great fun with the character. The most memorable, if also the most bizarre, delineation of the Sheriff of Nottingham on screen is undoubtedly that of Alan Rickman in *Robin Hood: Prince of Thieves*.

However, even the villainous Sheriff is not entirely beyond fictional rehabilitation. In 1992, the American writer Richard Kluger, a Pulitzer Prize winner for his non-fiction, published a novel which turned the legend on its head and made the Sheriff the embattled and misunderstood hero of his narrative. The outlaw Robin Hood is only peripheral to the story. *The Sheriff of Nottingham* focuses on the real historical figure of Philip Mark, and Kluger makes him a protagonist of genuine moral complexity. Faced with the difficulties of an embezzling servant and an unfaithful wife, the Sheriff is for once the character who gains our sympathies.

Alan a Dale

The minstrel Alan-a-Dale is a relatively late addition to the Merry Men, appearing for the first time in a seventeenth-century ballad entitled 'Robin Hood and Allin a Dale'. After first taking his bow as a cheery young man who did 'frisk it over the plain/And chanted a roundelay', Alan is a thwarted lover when seen the next day by Robin and his men. The woman he loves is being forced against her will to marry an elderly knight. The outlaws take a liking to Alan and agree to help him, invading the church where the marriage is taking place and making sure that the girl weds her true love. Alan-a-Dale was soon established as a regular member of the outlaw band and he has featured in most of the versions of the legend, both in print and on the screen, in the last century and a half. He has usually been relegated to the role of supporting player, although the ballad story of his love and marriage is repeated, with variations, in many of the children's Robin Hood books published in the twentieth century. In two re-tellings in different media in the last decade, he has been more prominent than usual. As played by Joe Armstrong in the 2006 BBC series, he has lost all his musical ability and become a small-time thief. He claims to come from Rochdale (hence his name) and joins the outlaws after Robin rescues him from hanging. With the unfolding of the story, he becomes a more complex character than the cheery songsmith most frequently portrayed. He turns traitor to his fellow merry men at one point before later returning to the fold and his internal debate about where his true loyalties lie provides the motive force behind the plots of several episodes. In Angus Donald's novel *Outlaw* and its sequels, Alan is the narrator of the book and, although he retains his minstrel skills, he is also a warrior who travels to the Holy Land with Robin and wreaks much bloody havoc there.

Much the Miller's Son

Like Little John and Will Scarlet, Much the Miller's Son is named as one of Robin's followers in the earliest of the ballads. In the Gest, he is present at the capture of Sir Richard at the Lee and takes part in the archery contest. In 'Robin Hood and the Monk', a ballad notable for the casual violence shown by Robin and his men, Much kills a page boy in order to prevent him bearing witness to the murder of the monk of the title. He is sometimes called 'Midge' in other ballads and it is this name that Howard Pyle appropriates for use in one of the stories in his 1883 book *The Merry Adventures of Robin Hood*. Much is more or less ever present in film and TV versions of the Robin Hood legend, although he rarely has a major role to play. In any scene involving the Merry Men, he is usually the one on the edge of the group, grinning gormlessly and awaiting his opportunity to deliver the one or two lines the scriptwriter has allotted him. The exceptions to this rule are two TV series. In *Robin of Sherwood* in the 1980s, Much (played by Peter Llewellyn Williams) is the simple-minded son of the miller who takes in Robin when he is a boy and he becomes a kind of foster brother in regular need of Robin's protection. In the more recent BBC series, Much is no longer a miller's son but has been transformed by the writers into Robin's manservant and fellow fighter in the Crusades. Played by Sam Troughton (grandson of Patrick Troughton who was the very first TV Robin in 1953), he is portrayed as both comic relief and the outlaw leader's closest and most loyal comrade. Adam Thorpe takes the story from 'Robin Hood and the Monk' as the basis for some of the pivotal events in his 2009 novel Hodd and the narrator of the newly-discovered medieval manuscript at the heart of the book turns out to be Much, although the character is very different from the traditional portrait of him. In the last few years, Much has also taken centre stage in an award-winning webcomic by Steve LeCouilliard. Although Robin can never remember his name correctly ('This is Mike the Mule-Skinner', he says, introducing him to the rest of the gang), Much becomes one of the merry men, nursing an unrequited passion for Maid Marian and being forced by Will Scarlet into a succession of improbable money-making schemes that usually end with him standing on the Sheriff of Nottingham's gallows, awaiting a last-minute rescue.

Sir Guy of Gisbourne

Introduced in the early ballad usually entitled 'Robin Hood and Guy of Gisborne', this character is the most frequently named of Robin's opponents other than the Sheriff of Nottingham. His name probably derives from either the village known today as Gisburn, once in the West Riding of Yorkshire but now in Lancashire, or possibly Guisborough in the North Riding. In the ballad, Sir Guy is a bounty hunter who has been hired by the Sheriff to track down Robin. The outlaw leader chances upon him in Sherwood, curiously clad in a horse's hide outfit (a detail that has suggested to some scholars that the character entered the Robin Hood story from an older narrative tradition involving ritual disguise), and the two men fight. Robin kills Guy and mutilates his body. Although he is a corpse at the end of the ballad, Sir Guy has been resurrected many times over the years and he has often played the part of Robin's brutish rival for the love of Maid Marian.

He is regularly portrayed in film and TV versions of the stories. Occasionally, as in the 1938 Warner Brothers film in which he is played by Basil Rathbone, he takes the role of chief villain from the Sheriff of Nottingham but he is more often shown as the Sheriff's nasty but none too bright sidekick. Robert Addie, for example, in *Robin of Sherwood*, plays him as the blunt military man, perennial butt of the more sophisticated baddies who have brains as well as brawn. In a clever twist, the consequences of which are never fully explored, Addie's character is revealed in the third season of the series as the illegitimate son of the Earl of Huntingdon and therefore the half-brother of Jason Connery's Robin. By far the most interesting and complex portrayal of Sir Guy is that of Richard Armitage in the BBC series that began in 2006. Intense and darkly handsome, Armitage plays the character as an apparent villain who nonetheless is always teetering on the brink of decency. His tormented love for Marian offers him a redemption which fate and his own failings are forever snatching from him. In the course of two series, the deeply ambivalent relationship between Gisborne and Marian, although it ends in tragedy, is markedly more compelling than her wishy-washy love affair with Jonas Armstrong's Robin.

Further Reading

Many of the poems, plays and novels about Robin that have been published over the last five centuries have already been mentioned in the main body of this book. I am not proposing to repeat them all in this section on 'Further Reading'. Listed below instead are a number of titles which look at the outlaw as historical figure or cultural icon or both. All of them proved useful and interesting when I was writing this book. Readers who want to learn more about Robin than I have been able to include in a Pocket Essential should search them out.

Baldwin, David, *Robin Hood: The English Outlaw Unmasked*, Stroud: Amberley Publishing, 2010

Bellamy, John, *Robin Hood: An Historical Enquiry*, London: Croom Helm, 1984

Bradbury, Jim, *Robin Hood*, Stroud: Amberley Publishing, 2010

Cawthorne, Nigel, *A Brief History of Robin Hood*, London: Robinson, 2010

Davis, John Paul, *Robin Hood: The Unknown Templar*, London: Peter Owen, 2009

Doel, Fran & Geoff, *Robin Hood: Outlaw or Greenwood Myth*, Stroud, Tempus Publishing, 2000

Hahn, Thomas (ed), *Robin Hood in Popular Culture*, Cambridge: D. S. Brewer, 2000

Holt, JC, *Robin Hood*, London: Thames & Hudson, 1982

Keen, Maurice, *Outlaws of Medieval Legend*, London: Routledge, 1961

Knight, Stephen, *Robin Hood: A Mythic Biography*, Ithaca, NY: Cornell University Press, 2003

Knight, Stephen (ed), *Robin Hood: An Anthology of Scholarship and Criticism*, Cambridge, DS Brewer, 1999

Matthews, John, *Robin Hood: Green Lord of the Wildwood*, Oxford: Gothic Image, 1993

Phillips, Graham & Keatman, Martin, *Robin Hood: The Man Behind the Myth*, London: Michael O'Mara, 1995

Pollard, AJ, *Imagining Robin Hood*, London: Routledge, 2004

Potter, Lois, *Playing Robin Hood; The Legend as Performance in Five Centuries*, Newark, DE: University of Delaware Press

Singman, Jeffrey, *Robin Hood: The Shaping of the Legend*, London: Greenwood Press, 1998

Index

Index

Index

Index

Index

Index